MW01094642

the art of
CHOICE

MAKING CHANGES THAT COUNT
IN WORK AND LIFE

TERRY WARREN

Copyright © 2021 Terry Warren.
https://warrenexecutivecoach.com

Quotes from individuals interviewed are used with permission. Identifying details in case studies have been changed.

All rights reserved. No part of this publication may be reproduced, distributed, or transmitted in any form or by any means, including photocopying, recording, or other electronic or mechanical methods, without the prior written permission of the publisher, except in the case of brief quotations embodied in critical reviews and certain other noncommercial uses permitted by copyright law. This book should not be construed as legal or therapeutic advice. At time of publication, all web links were active. For permission requests, write to the publisher, addressed "Attention: Permissions Coordinator," at the address below.

ISBN: 978-1-95386529-8 (Paperback)
ISBN: 978-1-95386530-4 (eBook)

Library of Congress Control Number: 2021907678

Books Fluent
3014 Dauphine Street
New Orleans, LA
70117

Cover Design: Bruce Gore | Gore Studio Inc.
Typesetting: Stewart A. Williams

Dedication

For my grandchildren, who encourage me about
the future. You are each uniquely gifted by God.
Use those gifts to make a difference in the world.
May you love well, serve well, lead well, make
good choices, and honor God in all you do.

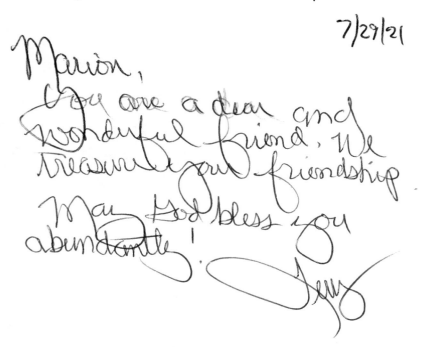

7/29/21

Marion,

You are a dear and
wonderful friend, We
treasure your friendship

May God bless you
abundantly!

Jerry

"May the God of hope fill you with all joy and peace in believing, so that by the power of the Holy Spirit you may abound in hope."
—ROMANS 15:13 (ESV)

ACKNOWLEDGMENTS

First and foremost, I thank God for all His blessings, including the opportunity to share this book with you. Secondly, I want to acknowledge the constant encouragement of my wife, Beverly. Whether it was for this book, my career in general, or my art, she has been there to tell me I am more capable than I believe. On a very real basis this book would have never been published without the incredible partnership with my editor, Amy Lyles Wilson. She knew exactly how to keep pushing me forward. I am especially grateful to the twenty-one leaders who generously gave me time from their busy schedules to be interviewed as part of my research on the topic of choice. Each story was inspirational to me. As an executive coach, I have also had my own coach at various times. I am grateful to Stephen McGhee, who dramatically changed how I think about coaching, and to Pat White and Pamela Richarde, who served as my mentor coaches. And finally, I am grateful to my clients. What you have achieved through intentional choices is incredible. Thank you for inspiring me.

CONTENTS

INTRODUCTION

Plenty of us sense that we need to make a big change in our lives, yet we just can't seem to make it happen. Maybe we're scared; maybe we don't have all the information we need; maybe we can't imagine what options exist for us. Maybe we've been told "no" so many times we don't allow ourselves to dream of a "yes."

How can we move past hesitancy and inaction and toward fulfillment and satisfaction? How can we develop the courage to pursue our goals? We can start by being honest with ourselves and taking action. We can start by learning from those who have gone before us, and by looking to leaders who make effective decisions.

What is one baby step you could take today that would move you toward what you want?

If you have not seen the movie *What About Bob?* (Touchstone, 1991), I suggest you check it out. It features Bill Murray, who, as Bob, is essentially confined to his apartment by multiple phobias. His exhausted therapist refers him to the egotistical Dr. Leo Marvin (Richard Dreyfus) who believes that his book, *Baby Steps,* will make him a household name. Bob reads the book, takes some "baby steps" out of his apartment, and is amazed at his progress. So amazed, in fact, that he then latches on to Dr. Marvin in such a way that drives Dr. Marvin crazy. You have to see the film to get the rest of the story, but to me, the underlying lesson for all of us is that any significant change can happen by starting with baby steps.

Every day we wake up with a choice about how we will view that day. Change is a choice. As an executive coach, seeing people over the years who wanted to make a life-altering change but were frustrated by not having the tools—or the confidence—to make the pivotal moves drove me to write this book. What I want for you is an understanding of, and appreciation for, the power you have within you to make choices that can transform your life and career. I want to share some stories of people who have successfully made major shifts, and pose some thought-provoking questions to get you moving toward your goals.

Intentionality, commitment, persistent actions, and accountability partners will get you unstuck and lead you successfully to transformational change. Additionally, as a Christian, I consider prayer to be a necessary and integral part of the choices I make.

At one point in my life, I had a job that proved to be the worst job of my entire career. It was in a smaller company where there was essentially no support. The job required extremely long hours and my working nights and weekends. On the job, I was required to learn to support myself in ways I had never had to do before. I could not imagine at the time how this experience would ever be useful to me, as much of the work seemed to be menial for the level at which I was being paid.

Some twenty-five years later, I was volunteering as a mentor and consultant for a youth ministry in Ukraine. Our group was meeting one day in Kiev, when I realized there was a skill I had learned in that difficult job two decades earlier that applied to the problem the organization faced now. That gave me a keen understanding of a phrase I have come to truly appreciate: "God does not waste any experience." That experience, and many more over my long career, taught me that even your bad choices offer experiences and warnings that will benefit you at some point in the future. The key is not to stay stuck in the mistake or to feel that any experience was a waste of your time.

After coaching high-level achievers for a few years, I saw a pattern among my clients. Every client who made an intentional choice along with a personal commitment to change—succeeded. *One hundred percent success.* In short, they made a choice with intention and commitment, and they were successful. You can do the same. I'd like to think these people made changes because I'm a fabulous coach, but I suspect most of the credit goes to their realizing and harnessing the power they had within themselves to enact transformational, positive choices.

Here's what I mean when I talk about powerful or life-altering choices:

- Changing a behavior that does not serve you well
- Believing what is possible
- Shedding a belief that holds you back
- Finding balance
- Learning to regulate emotions
- Deciding to delegate
- Letting go of some of the control
- Becoming more self-aware
- Being confident in yourself

On the surface, some of these may not seem life altering, but in fact they are.

In a conversation with one of my clients, we discussed how he found balance in his life despite having been promoted from a senior leadership role in a global organization to an even bigger role that had the potential to become all-consuming. Unfortunately, he had not achieved balance in his former position, and he wanted to handle his life differently in his new job. He knew he needed to develop boundaries from the start before he established behaviors that would be hard to undo later.

We talked about various actions he might take, such as delegating appropriately, realizing his attendance wasn't required at every meeting, and giving himself permission to carve out "me" time. Later, when I asked him if these action items were what really made his efforts successful, his response was "no." Instead, he said, at the very core was his *choice* to find balance. So, although the steps we outlined *contributed* to his finding balance, at the root it was his conscious decision that made all the difference. His desire to find balance became important enough to him to be intentional, committed, and accountable toward that goal.

I wanted to find out if what I was observing in my own clients—their making powerful choices with success—had affected the lives and careers of other leaders across different industries. How had they navigated change in their careers? Had intentionality, commitment, and accountability played a role in their success? Did they have additional suggestions to offer those who needed to take the next step?

My original plan was to speak to a few leaders, blend what I learned from them with what I had gleaned from working with my own clients, and develop a speech I could present to businesses, nonprofit organizations, and civic groups to help their teams make effective choices.

I began my research in Nashville, Tennessee, where I have lived and worked for most of my career and where I'm surrounded by successful people. I asked each interviewee to tell me about a time when he or she made a career choice they believed to be so important that they never looked back after making their decision. I think about this as a "jumping off the cliff" kind of choice and not merely a New Year's resolution made after feeling guilty about overeating during the holidays. I wanted to know how they stayed committed to their choice once it was made. I also asked for advice I could share with others.

After several of these conversations, I realized there really was something behind the power we have within us to make life and career choices and see them through. I knew what I was learning needed to be shared on a broader basis than just a few speeches I might give. A book seemed like the best way to share what I learned.

The first interviews were so interesting I decided to ask each person to recommend someone else for me to meet. Over the next twelve months, I interviewed a total of twenty-one different leaders from a wide variety of industries. All of them had at least one inspirational and educational story about a choice they made and the impact it had on their life and career.

My goal is not to share each and every interview, but to present common threads and themes in the hope that one or more might be relevant to a choice you know you need to make. In addition, throughout the book you will find case studies as examples of how people make effective choices.

I have used the word "art" in the title of this book because, while there is science to support how we can stimulate different parts of the brain when making intentional choices, there is far more art than science involved when we decide on changes that really count in our life. I'm also a visual artist, as well as an executive coach, and over the years I have come to appreciate how art informs life and life informs art. You'll find that I draw on my work and my art in the book.

While training to be an executive coach, I learned that stories can be an important coaching tool. The key is to keep them short and relevant to the current discussion. Now that I have been coaching for several years, I have truly seen the value of stories. I find that my clients can relate to what we're discussing if I have a story to illustrate a point, or to cause them to think about a similar situation in their own lives.

In short, this is a book of stories. Stories of how successful leaders—people just like you and me—made their changes count.

What changes do you need to make?

CHAPTER 1

Early Choices

If you want to have a better performance than the crowd,
you must do things differently from the crowd.
—JOHN TEMPLETON

When I began this journey in order to better understand the power people have within themselves to make successful life-altering choices, I also began thinking about the critical choices I have made along the way. In retrospect, there have been many. Some, I would classify as simple yet transformational, and others as truly life changing.

I grew up in a small town in Tennessee, where the majority of people worked hard to make ends meet. I was blessed to be part of a loving family with strong values, but we struggled financially. My parents went to school through the fifth grade, and my father passed away when I was fourteen.

Dad had many different jobs, but most of my memories

are around his work as a carpenter. I remember his telling me, "Son, I want you to be a pencil pusher and not do all of this hard work that I have to do as a carpenter." I think, in some ways, his advice planted the seed in my mind to find another way to make a living. Back then, I thought he was telling me he didn't want me to work as hard as he did, but I now think he was really saying he knew I was a terrible carpenter and I would never make a living that way.

Perhaps my first big choice was the choice to go in a different direction than my father. But what direction would I choose? My impression, from watching television and from observing the few people in my town who were what I would call "successful" in business, was the importance of a college education. I felt that going to college would open up opportunities I otherwise would not have. I also had this inner desire to see what options were available to people in larger cities. No one in my family had gone to college, but I knew I had to go.

With some research, I determined that if I could earn and save money while in high school, get a scholarship and a contribution from my mother, and then become a co-op student after the first college year, I could afford to go. My mother had worked in a factory most of her life. She certainly was not opposed to my going to college, but she was reluctant to loan me money because she had not been able to support my older siblings in such a way. In the end, though, she did agree to co-sign a loan for the first year.

I made the choice to go to Tennessee Technological University (Tennessee Tech) and major in engineering, because it made sense to me and I had friends who had done that. Additionally, Tennessee Tech offered the opportunity for me to be a co-op student, which would allow me to go to school for a year, work a year to pay for the following year, go to school a year, and so on. It seemed the obvious choice, and I think it was a good one.

My accountability for seeing this through was largely self-imposed, along with my desire to not disappoint my mother. I was blessed that the head of the Department of Industrial Engineering at Tennessee Tech, Dr. Sid Gilbreath, saw something in me I did not see. He became a constant source of encouragement and pushed me to places I would never have thought possible. I am forever grateful to Sid.

While my next intentional choice might not have appeared to be life changing, it shifted everything for me on both professional and personal levels. I wanted to be the kind of person who could drop into any social or work situation and feel comfortable in my interactions with others. Quite simply, I wanted to be able to meet people where they were, and align my conversations and actions accordingly. To make that happen, though, I first had to convince myself I had something to offer.

Having grown up poor in a working-class family in a small town, I had no issue relating to people from similar backgrounds. But learning to be comfortable around the well-educated, wealthy, or senior executive leaders would take a lot of work. For starters, I needed to develop self-confidence.

My encourager, Sid, was also my role model for this endeavor. He was a smart man who had the gift of connecting with all kinds of folks, be they high-level professionals, school support staff, or townspeople. I witnessed him treat everyone he encountered with genuine interest, even if they had little in common. He was able, with ease, to engage anyone who crossed his path with sincere attentiveness and compassion. I wanted to be more like Sid.

To protect the guilty I won't provide details, but I remember a time when our school's industrial engineering professional group traveled to another city for a conference, with Sid as our leader. I witnessed a situation that I worried might escalate into a fight between Sid and several members of another college's football team. To my utter amazement, Sid not only diffused the situation, but he was also treated to drinks by the other players. I remember many fun moments from that trip, but watching Sid in action solidified my desire to be like him. I wanted to handle my future life situations with the same awareness and skill. A choice to change the way you conduct yourself in the world is not an easy one, and it takes time and intentionality. But it's a choice worth making.

Another transformational choice for me was going to graduate school after I finished college. Just as in my undergraduate days, I had to work part time and get a scholarship. The consulting work I did in grad school at the Georgia Institute of Technology (Georgia Tech) exposed me to more professional opportunities. After completing my master's degree in industrial management, I landed my first job "pushing a pencil." I believe my father would have been pleased.

Not all of my choices have been good, and many of them had difficult consequences. One involved leaving a comfortable career with a large company and moving out of state to take on a role that turned out to be devastating. There are many reasons the move was not a good one, and it lasted only a year. But instead of dwelling on what went wrong in the short term, I prefer to appreciate what became possible in the long term.

When I realized this particular move was not going to work, I had to make another choice: I committed to finding a new opportunity. Years later, I realized I had learned a lot from the misstep. Sometimes, knowing what you don't want to do, or where you don't want to be, is a good start to discovering where you do belong.

I would like to say that this was the only bad choice I ever made, but that would not be true. Instead, I'll take the approach of my friend Steve Lynn, who says, "Fail forward." If we choose to do that, we can leverage failure to build success for the future.

I first met Steve when we were both industrial engineering undergraduate students at Tennessee Tech. Steve was there on a tennis scholarship. Like me, he'd grown up poor in a small, rural community. Throughout what became a distinguished career on his part, he had many big successes and a number of failures.

Steve was the first person I interviewed when I began my research for this book. As we sat in his comfortable home office, I asked him to tell me about some choices he'd had to make that were difficult but that ultimately had a positive impact on his career. I learned a lot from listening to Steve and watching his body language. When he recalled a difficult choice he'd had to make, he leaned forward and became clearly excited about the memory of that choice.

Steve had faced a life-altering choice while still in high school. A local businessman who had befriended Steve suggested that he needed to spend time with a different peer group. We all know that high school is rife with peer pressure.

That decision to separate from a certain group of friends wasn't easy for Steve, but he was determined to make something of his life. Later, the local businessman helped Steve get the tennis scholarship that led him to Tennessee Tech.

At one point in his career, Steve was also fired from his job. Sometimes, we look at highly successful people and we assume they've had it "easy," so to speak. But this is not actually true most of the time. Indeed, Steve would tell you that his emotions and ego were pretty deflated when he was fired. But, because of his strong faith, he chose not to live in that failure or let that failure define his future. When we make choices that don't work out, we have the opportunity to take what may be an even more important next step: the decision not to *live* in the disappointment.

Early in my career, I realized I had always been a goal-oriented person. Setting new goals and checking them off was part of my DNA. At some point, I set a goal to become the CEO of a company before I turned forty-five. A year or two before that birthday, I made it. I became CEO of a subsidiary of a larger company. Hitting that goal felt great, at least for a time. After a couple of years, though, I had this odd feeling that something was missing. Soon, I realized I had not yet imagined a new goal for myself. I had achieved everything I had set out to do, but that did not seem like enough. I began to wonder, "What is this *life* thing really all about?"

About that time, a friend recommended the book *Half-time*, by Bob Buford, a successful executive who'd made the shift from success to significance. In short, the book is about deciding what is most important in life and adjusting your focus accordingly. In reading Buford's words, I was inspired to make my own shift toward what was most important to me.

From the standpoint of achieving my own goals, I certainly felt successful, but I did not feel significant. At that time, there was a lot of uncertainty in our company, which only exacerbated my discontent. The realization that there was more to life than being considered "successful" by society's standards forced a major change in my life, one that caused me to focus on having an impact—being *significant* rather than merely seeking more of what others label as success. It wasn't easy or quick, but I was committed to making the shift. A key ingredient for me was accepting God as the one in control. Interestingly, as I began to concentrate on significance over success, opportunities came my way that afforded me both. I believe that God orchestrated this.

I soon became involved with a local nonprofit that worked with at-risk, inner city youth; an organization making a real difference. I also spent time reflecting on why I got up and went to work every day. What would be important enough to me that I would enjoy doing it, regardless of potential recognition or earnings, in the next phase of my life? And, maybe even more important, what did I want to leave as my legacy?

For me, the driving force for going to work was feeling that I was helping people, be they co-workers or clients. I felt significant when I served others. I wanted to do my best with the task at hand and not focus on the next rung on the ladder. As it turned out, this was a common thread among most of the successful leaders I interviewed. They, too, wanted to "grow where they were planted" without obsessing over their next move.

Four years before I was set to retire from my corporate life, I faced another transformational choice. I knew I was not the retiring type, but what would I do, and who would I be, in my next chapter?

I spoke with my company's leadership about my desire to do *one more thing* there that would make a difference before I retired, but at the time we didn't know what that might be. I spent the next year talking to different people about what I might do. Although a year seems like a long time, I felt it was essential, because the outcome for me was that important.

During this time of inquiry and soul searching, I heard an executive coach speak at a corporate meeting. I instantly knew that coaching was what I wanted to do. I pulled the coach aside after the meeting and peppered him with questions. Soon, I began the process of speaking with a number of other coaches (executive coaches, life coaches, and so on) to see what I could learn. I asked such questions as, "What is the best thing about being a coach? The worst? What education and training are required?"

After completing my research, I went back to my corporate leaders.

"I've found what I can do for the company before I retire," I said. "I'm going to train as an executive coach, and I will pay for my training while continuing to work for you. I only ask that you let me coach employees when it comes time for me to put in the coaching hours required by the training."

They agreed, without hesitation. The day after my retirement from the company in which I had served twenty-eight years, I opened my own coaching practice. I am happy to report that my former employer remains a client, and my practice has far exceeded my expectations. Without a doubt, this choice was one of the best I've ever made.

Yet, there have been crises of confidence along the way. In coaching school, you learn that coaching is never about you. You should not evaluate your own performance in a coaching session, because the time is concentrated solely on the client. All true, but every coach I know—if they're being honest—will admit to doubting their skill on a given day. Additionally, although much of my career had been spent reporting to or working closely with CEOs and senior officers in large global companies, I went through a crisis of confidence around whether I was good enough as a coach to work with leaders at all levels.

Enter *my* coach, Stephen McGhee.

Yes, good coaches have coaches. Stephen adeptly helped me shift my thinking from "performing as a coach to a place of coaching out of a total commitment to serving my clients." This seemingly small shift in my mindset released me from worrying about evaluating my coaching to having the freedom of serving my clients in the moment, so they might more readily find their own solutions from within.

To resolve my crisis of confidence about working with top leaders, Stephen instructed me to watch the movie *Sully: Miracle on the Hudson* (Warner Brothers, 2016), and then tell him where I saw myself in the main character. You may know the movie, which is based on the book *Highest Duty* by Chesley "Sully" Sullenberger and Jeffrey Zaslow, and tells the true story of Sully making an emergency plane landing on the Hudson River in 2009. All crew and passengers survived. There really were several similarities between Sully and me:

- Forty-plus years of experience in our craft
- Near, or already in, retirement

- Instincts that guide us in situations never faced before
- Self-talk around "my airplane" (or, knowing when we need to take control)

Throughout the latter part of my career, I was blessed to be the trusted advisor to many senior leaders, most of whom were my bosses. They found that they could be open with me, because they knew I would not share our conversations. Between working with these leaders and coaching high-level leaders, I have realized how many of us privately struggle with confidence. I have no scientific information that supports this, but my theory is that crises of confidence occur when we come back down from a "mountaintop" success experience, or when we allow a past failure to become more significant in our minds than it should be.

Although today I still have occasional moments of self-doubt, they are rare. People who know me now would be shocked to hear that, for most of my life, I suffered from lack of confidence. I'm grateful to have learned the tools and developed the temperament for a strong sense of self.

There are two key things I want you to take away from this chapter: You *do* have the power and ability to make transformational choices if you make them intentionally, pursue them with commitment and passion, and engage with accountability partners. And, you will likely need to keep making the same choice until the desired change becomes a whole new habit.

What choices have gotten you where you are today?

CHAPTER 2

Grow Where You Are Planted

Don't limit yourself. Many people limit themselves to what they think they can do. You can go as far as your mind lets you. What you believe, remember, you can achieve.
— MARY KAY ASH

The phrase "career builder" implies action and choices. A house does not get built without a good design and a builder who chooses the proper materials and puts them together skillfully. Builders must rely on others to help, but they must also take actions that lead to the right end result.

Like the house builder, your success in building and maintaining a fulfilling career requires your active participation. Some people prefer to work under the radar, having little desire to advance. There is nothing wrong with that. In my experience, every organization needs team members who are content right where they are. But if you secretly hope or assume that someone will eventually notice you and move you up in the organization without your having to make yourself known, I think you'll be disappointed.

I have also met people on the far end of fast-track eagerness. As an employer, I have over the years interviewed many people who expressed a desire for the job for which they were applying, but made it clear they expected to move up quickly to a "bigger" job.

"Hey," they might say, "How long before I'm named CEO?" I suspect you know people who fit in this category. I'm pretty sure I never hired any of them. If I did, I bet I regretted it.

If I had a magic formula for guaranteed career advancement or life satisfaction, I'd be rich enough to buy my dream home on Cape Cod Bay. But, what I do have to offer you are suggestions and insights I've gleaned through more than forty years of working in business, and almost a decade of serving as an executive coach. Unless you are at the end of your career, you will need to make important choices in order to move to the next level, whatever that may look like for you. And for those nearing retirement, you have important choices to make as well, such as how to make the most of the rest of your life.

Ask yourself, "Am I going to let others manage my career, or am I going to make sure I'm an active participant in managing it? Am I concentrating on giving my best to whatever position I have right now, or am I focusing on the future at the cost of the present?"

If you attend to your current job well, and voluntarily take on additional duties as appropriate, your actions will be noticed. New opportunities will eventually emerge. Simply put: do the next right thing, and do it well.

There are a lot of good leadership books out there, and some of my favorites are listed in the Recommended Resources section at the back of the book. But in my opinion, the Bible is the best leadership book ever published. It has something to say about how we should view our current roles.

> Whatever you do, work heartily, as for the Lord
> and not for men.
> —Colossians 3:23 (ESV)

> For I have learned in whatever situation I am to
> be content.
> —Philippians 4:11 (ESV)

I recently had a conversation with a client who had been offered a new position with her current employer. At the same time, she thought she was being considered for another role in the company that might become available in the future. Should she take the new job offered right then, or hold out for the potential future position? Up to that point, her career path had been one of working hard and taking on assignments that stretched her. She had always performed each task well. Knowing her track record of solid performance, I challenged her to consider whether the best opportunity might just be the one right in front of her at the moment. She chose the one in front of her, and over the next few years, she was given increasingly larger roles. Her pattern was to do whatever she was doing well, and appropriately share successes; which, in turn, caused her to be tapped for bigger and better roles as time went on.

Following that same route I'd suggested to my client turned out to be a common strategy among the professionals I interviewed.

One leader, Ron Samuels, who was near the end of a successful career in banking, said he had not sought out leadership opportunities throughout his younger life. He was happy to do whatever he was doing at the time, and to do it really well. But based on his performance, he was asked to step into leadership roles, which opened up additional opportunities he had not expected. I am sure he had dreams of long-term success, but my sense is that he approached "being successful" as doing very well with whatever he was tasked with at the time. Eventually, Ron realized that he was a natural leader and, in fact, his leadership abilities earned him great respect over the years.

When I interviewed Bob Fisher, president of Belmont University in Nashville, I discovered a fascinating example of not only growing—but also *thriving*—where you are planted. Bob was a vice president at a large public university when, unbeknownst to him, his university president recommended him to take the lead over at Belmont. But Bob wasn't convinced that a private institution was the right fit for him, thinking he might actually want to run a large public university one day. When Belmont first contacted Bob, he declined the offer. But Belmont's leadership did not give up.

Belmont's persistence, a lot of prayer by Bob, and his eventual feeling that Belmont seemed to be part of God's plan soon led him and his wife to accept the offer and move to Nashville from another state. Bob told me, "I just stepped out, took a little risk, and stepped out in faith…it's been a huge blessing."

Deciding to give his best wherever he was at the time,

Bob actually led the small university through a period of unprecedented growth and expansion. When Bob arrived, Belmont had 2,900 students. As of 2021 the year Bob retired, the school had more than 8,000.

Later on, when recruiters reached out to him about an opportunity to run a "big school," Bob said no—not even wanting to know the name of the institution. Instead, he continues to build a big school where he's planted. Bob's advice is to be "relentless" about your work and "press on when times are tough."

In my own career, there were many times when the next opportunity wasn't clear. When I got passed over for a particular job I wanted, I admit I was disappointed. I could have easily become discouraged or hopeless. But giving up was not an option in my mind.

Having the benefit of hindsight—with some forty-plus years of experience—I now see that there was a pattern to my career. The pattern was something like this: get a job and give it my best, keep my eyes open for new opportunity, become disappointed when I was unclear on what was next or was turned down for a role I wanted, keep performing at a high level nonetheless, and find a new opportunity—repeat. Most of the leaders I interviewed had a similar pattern. My experience, combined with the experience of the people I interviewed, exceeded six hundred years of lessons from which to draw. While not a complete list, here are a few themes that emerged around the idea of growing where you are planted:

- Be reliable and trustworthy
- Always give your best to whatever you are doing
- Develop your self-awareness

- Look for opportunities to demonstrate more of your skills
- Promote yourself without being boastful
- Make self-development and growth a lifetime pursuit

BE RELIABLE AND TRUSTWORTHY

I remember a conversation I had with my CEO when I was in the corporate world. There was a large project for which he was ultimately responsible, but he asked me to lead it for him. At various times along the way during my management of the project, I became frustrated because I could not get his attention or assistance even though the project was important to him. One day, I flew to New York to give him a progress report, and expressed my frustration that he didn't seem concerned.

"Do you worry a lot about the project?" he asked.

"I sure do," I said.

Though succinct, his response told me all I needed to know.

"Terry," he said, "if you are worried about it, then *I* do not need to be worried."

Be *that* reliable. Whatever you are asked to do, do it well and finish on time. You want a reputation for being competent and conscientious.

We all know people who like to talk about how much integrity they have and how trustworthy they are. For me, such boasting is a sure sign they do not possess either of those qualities. In business, a true indicator of integrity and trustworthiness is doing what you say you will do when you say you will do it, or giving advance notice of potential delays. We all know people who would never intentionally do anything immoral, illegal, or unethical. In these areas, they are models of integrity; yet some of these same people cannot be trusted in their professional lives to do what they say they will do when they say they will do it.

One of my coaching clients was a CEO who I knew to have high morals and strong ethics. As part of our work together, I interviewed a number of people at his company, including leadership and staff. Unfortunately, a common thread from the interviews revealed that the CEO was not considered trustworthy. I probed a bit to better understand why. It came down to the fact that he could not be relied on to do what he said he would do.

It can be that simple.

Always Give Your Best

Dave Jones has a successful career in the hospitality business. He started out as an assistant food and beverage director at a Holiday Inn, and built his entire career by doing his best, regardless of what he was doing. He moved up the ranks, helped launch a now prominent hotel brand, and served as president and chief executive officer of Gaylord Entertainment Company's Opryland Hospitality Group. He now has his own hotel development and management company. To illustrate always giving your best, Dave told me a story from his time with a major hotel firm.

"We got a new chairman, a sharp young guy," said Dave. "And he really believed in high potential people. I'm going along, really happy with what I'm doing, and he says, 'Well, I need you to walk away from operations,' which was like putting a sword in my side because I really enjoyed operations." His boss wanted Dave to take on a new responsibility.

"He wanted me to run a development division, which had four hundred fifty people made up of designers, architects, engineers, and so on. It was somewhat connected, but it was a whole new business."

Because Dave was now selling a different level of services to a different kind of client, it was a huge change for him. But he knew he had to do it in order to take another step in the company. And there were other times that Dave did his best with his current assignments in order to garner new challenges and increased growth. That kind of awareness and willingness served him well.

Choosing to give your best means you will need to stretch yourself. As a manager, I have led people who did good quality work in a timely fashion, but who lacked the edge their work needed to be their *best* work.

What is the edge that makes good work your best work? The edge that leaders look for in others? It's my belief that the edge is developed by people who proactively:

- Seek input from others before finalizing a solution
- Question if there is an even better way to approach a project
- Think about the long-term impact of potential solutions
- Recognize the best person to solve an issue may be someone else, then recommend that person with full support
- Always perform at a high level

Interviewee Milton Johnson hit the nail on the head when he said, "I feel there is a secret sauce in whatever position I had, which was to be the best at whatever job I was asked to do."

DEVELOP YOUR SELF-AWARENESS

In Act I, Scene III of Shakespeare's *Hamlet*, Polonius speaks these famous words to his son, Laetres:

This above all: to thine own self be true,
And it must follow, as the night the day,
Thou canst not then be false to any man.

How can you be true to yourself if you are not aware of who you are?

I am in the Executive Coaching Network for the Owen Graduate School of Management at Vanderbilt University. There, coaches are assigned to a number of first-year MBA students. It is so much fun to work with these bright young men and women.

Interviewing for summer internships proves to be a stressful time for the students. The focus of our coaching varies by student, but one of the common themes is preparing for those critical interviews. In the process, I ask them to write down what they consider special about themselves. Every human is uniquely designed. It is important for us to understand ourselves well so that we can leverage our distinctiveness to the benefit of a prospective company. Truly knowing yourself—your skills, your interests, your passions, your weaknesses, your blind spots—sets you apart whether you are interviewing for a job, seeking a promotion, contemplating retirement, or changing careers.

There are many ways to gain self-awareness. Following

are a few suggestions, but you'll need to put your own spin on them as you excavate your personality and your own experience.

Think back over your life and career to date, regardless of your age. List what you have done well, and then look for a word or two that describes each skill or strength. For example, if people with complex issues often come to you for help, you are likely a "problem solver." Maybe, when you look back, you see that in almost every situation you ended up being the leader. Then you can map out those leadership skills as examples for an employer.

Ron Samuels had a successful career in banking, including founding Avenue Bank and co-founding the Mid South School of Banking, now called the Barrett School of Banking, in Memphis. As we talked about his choices, he told me how, from his teenage years throughout his career, he was asked to lead almost everything in which he was involved, even though he hadn't sought leadership roles. Although he describes himself as "height challenged," along the way he was even asked to take the lead in some sports organizations—something he might not have imagined for himself. Don't let your perceived limitations hold you back. He gave every leadership role his best, which led to the next role, and the next.

There are many ways to increase your self-awareness, including such tools as personality and aptitude tests. Some assessments are designed to identify personality types and how different types interact. Others measure intelligence, and still others measure strengths and weaknesses. My go-to instrument, the Judgment Index, measures the strength of various indicators of good judgment and how well you balance the use of those indicators. Others you might consider include 360 reviews, Hogan Personality Inventory, DISC, and Myers-Briggs. You can also ask your family and friends to respond to such questions as, "What have you observed about me that you think I should do more or less of?" and, "Is there anything that I should start doing or stop doing?" This kind of feedback can help you know yourself better in order to position yourself for your next step.

LOOK FOR OPPORTUNITIES TO DEMONSTRATE MORE OF YOUR SKILLS

My experience has been that most people want to be led. So why not simply lead? You do not need formal authority to demonstrate leadership. I recently coached an MBA student who had historically taken on leadership in most groups in which he was involved. At the time, he was part of a multi-disciplinary team working on a service project in a different country. Because he did not want to appear presumptuous, he forced himself to focus on being a solid team member instead of inserting himself as the leader.

No one else stepped up to guide the team, however, and the project suffered. As we discussed this, he realized that the team actually needed his leadership skills. Opportunities like these are chances for you to demonstrate leadership without being labeled as the one in charge from the outset.

I once had a salesperson working for me who kept asking for a management job. "Over the next few months," I advised him, "find some way to demonstrate your leadership skills, and I will definitely consider you for future management roles." He never did take the initiative to look for opportunities to lead, unfortunately; and he never became a manager.

Most people in positions of authority are delighted with

people who come forward with ideas about better ways to do their jobs or who offer solutions for problems they've observed, assuming that the suggestions are presented in a constructive and professional manner. Even if your solutions are not implemented, such proactive thinking demonstrates your ability to work beyond your daily tasks.

Marty Dickens retired a few years ago after a successful career in the communications field. In our interview, he told me a number of stories about times where he had the opportunity to take on new challenges. One opportunity stood out for me as another way to illustrate seizing opportunities to demonstrate more of your skills.

His company had made the decision to expand its reach beyond the United States, as the owners wanted to set up partnerships in various regions of the world. Neither Marty nor his company had any international experience. They asked Marty to lead this effort and he agreed, despite having no prior experience. He had to trust that he could meet the challenge. He did this successfully, which then opened up higher level opportunities for the remainder of his career.

If you have ever ridden the Tube in London, you're familiar with the announcement that comes at every stop when the doors open. "Mind the gap" is simply a reminder to be aware of the space between the station platform and the train. Watch your step, in other words. In your work, you need to be on the lookout for the gaps—what needs to be done—and volunteer to do that on top of what you are already doing. Yes, there are times when you'll need to agree to take on more duties without expectation of additional pay or a new title. All the successful people I interviewed did that multiple times in their careers.

Promote Yourself
without Being Boastful

In my work as an executive coach, and really throughout my career, I have noticed concepts that, when misunderstood, tend to conjure up negative thoughts that hold us back. Case in point: self-promotion.

When most people think about self-promotion, they often consider it an act of blustery swagger. And we can all cite examples of people who only want to talk about themselves and their amazing accomplishments or skills. This type of shameless self-interest gives the whole concept of self-promotion a bad rap. However, if used properly, it is powerful and necessary for your career.

Bragging might be described as boasting, which involves exaggeration and excessive pride or vanity. At its root, bragging is about shining the spotlight on yourself.

Self-promotion, on the other hand, is about raising awareness of your skills, accomplishments (both individual and team), and competencies in ways that build a positive personal brand. In chapter eight of *What Got You Here Won't Get You There*, executive coach Marshall Goldsmith has several mottos and points of emphasis regarding self-promotion:

- "Do you think people will buy without a good advertising campaign?"
- "Be your own press secretary"
- "Treat every day as if it were a press conference in which your colleagues are judging you"
- "Behave as if every day was an opportunity to hit a home run"

To make self-promotion a natural part of who you are in the working world, consider these steps:

- Look at your motives
- Let go of negative views of self-promotion
- List your key accomplishments. What common threads made these possible?
- Think of times you appropriately recognized others under your leadership
- Volunteer to work on a project
- Inform your manager about your accomplishments rather than waiting for a performance review
- Stick to facts and avoid exaggerations
- Use storytelling to demonstrate your achievements

In his book *Let's All Make the Day Count: The Everyday Wisdom of Charlie Daniels*, Daniels says: "Self-confidence and conceit are two different things. Self-confidence is the assurance that through talent, experience, familiarity, and ability you can handle a certain situation or perform a certain task. Conceit is…false confidence based on competitiveness, braggadocio, and bluster."

MAKE SELF-DEVELOPMENT AND GROWTH A LIFETIME PURSUIT

I have long loved the title of Goldsmith's book, *What Got You Here Won't Get You There*. If you are looking to be in, or have been promoted to, a new role, I highly recommend the book. Goldsmith talks about how, sometimes, our success to date may not serve us well in a new role. "One of the greatest mistakes of successful people is the assumption, 'I behave this way and I achieve results. Therefore, I must be achieving results because I behave this way.'"

I have coached many leaders who, after being successful in technical roles, are asked to step into management. This requires a significant shift in both what they do and who they are. Milton Johnson, chairman and chief executive officer of a large healthcare company, rose through the ranks of internal auditing to chief financial officer, and assumed he would be in that position until he retired. One day, though, he learned that the chief executive officer wanted him to take over when he left. This would require him to be more outgoing, more involved with employees, and to be the public face of the company. In short—he would have to change his way of being in the world.

He needn't try to replicate the executive he was replacing, as all of us should honor our own authentic styles. But he did have to make some changes as he learned what was required of him in his new position. He would ask for help when he needed it, and would learn from practice.

Major General Jerry Grizzle, PhD, president/superintendent of the New Mexico Military Institute, is a wonderful example of self-development and growth. Given his title, you might assume that Jerry spent all of his adult life in the military, but that is not his story. He served many years rising through the ranks in the Army National Guard while pursuing his business career, and he was deputy commander of the 45th Infantry Brigade of the Oklahoma National Guard during their response to the Alfred P. Murrah Federal Building bombing of 1995. After 9/11, he took command of Joint Task Force Civil Support.

Throughout his business career, which was focused

mainly within the food sector, Jerry sought opportunities to develop himself, all the while working long hours to perform his job well. Along the way, Jerry earned his master's and doctorate degrees, and he now enjoys teaching in addition to his other responsibilities.

Regarding change, Jerry said, "It's been my impression, both in the military and in business, that many people don't realize something needs to be changed, and that's bad for them and their organization. You have to come to the realization and understanding that something needs to change. It is difficult, but you need to be honest and realistic. One of the principles in the military is to know yourself and seek self-improvement. You've got to be your own self critic. You have got to start with yourself."

As you have learned from the examples above, there are many ways to seek additional learning and growth, whether personal or professional. I like to approach this from a practical standpoint.

For starters, have an insatiable curiosity. And I believe that if you are not stretching, you are shrinking. If you are not going forward, you are going backward. Make your own opportunities to learn. Be observant. I am both an executive coach and a visual artist. And a key ingredient for my growth in business and in art has been studying those who have already achieved what I aspire to. Ask yourself such questions as:

- What characteristics do I admire most about the successful folks?
- What characteristics do I least admire? And what do I want to be sure I don't do?

- What are the primary gaps between my current skills and behaviors and theirs?
- What do I need to learn or be able to do that I am not doing today?
- Where might I go to develop my skills? And who can help me?
- Which people around me continue to grow? How do they approach lifetime learning?

Being an artist who prefers painting landscapes in a realistic style, it is often necessary for me to paint water. I've struggled with how to capture the movement of oceans and streams. My art mentor paints magnificent water, so I asked him to help. He told me that it was easy to paint believable water, and challenged me to paint ocean waves hitting a beach. It was not as hard as I thought, but I was a long way from consistency. Other than technique, the gap between our results was that he had painted water some ten thousand times.

He always told me that, in order to become a better artist, I should "paint more." So, I do.

What do you need to do more of?

WHAT GIVES YOU ENERGY?

The CEO of a holding company built his subsidiaries through hard work and determination. He was known for making good, quick decisions. He came to me for coaching at a time when he needed to transition from being the top salesperson to becoming CEO, after the current CEO left.

This was a challenging transition for him, because he did not want people to think of him as the CEO—but rather as one of them. In our first meeting, the major decision he faced overshadowed his transition to CEO, although that was also important to him. The big choice he had to make was whether to accept an outside investor's significant amount of cash for partial ownership of his company, or to continue to grow his company organically. As I mentioned, this man had a history of strong decision-making, but he seemed stuck on this one. As I asked him questions about the pros and cons of each choice, I was glad we were in the same room so that I could observe his body language. When he spoke of one alternative, the level of excitement and energy was relatively low. When he spoke about the other, he became visibly excited.

After a long discussion, I told him I thought he had actually already made the decision, based on what I saw from his different energy levels around each alternative. He considered that for a minute or so before agreeing. He decided, at that moment, to pursue the choice that gave him the most energy. But, true to his character as a competent business- man, he proceeded with caution, reserving the right to exit the deal if need be. This is just one example of the importance of paying attention both to what gives you energy and what drains you.

CHAPTER 3

Choose Who You Will Be

For extraordinary people, most days are filled with seemingly ordinary tasks. But they enjoy brief, shining moments of victory along the way—and those moments imbue the other moments with a sense of purpose that gives joy and meaning to life.
—STEPHEN MCGHEE

In another chapter, I talked about getting to know yourself. How can you decide who you will be if you don't know who you are? When I consider this, I automatically think about being authentic, about leading from a place of authenticity.

Many years ago, one of my co-workers would walk up to me periodically, straighten my tie, and say, "Be somebody." In the context of place and time, my associate was saying that if you were to "be somebody," you best be neat and tidy. Our company had a clear expectation about how one should dress. One morning, every employee found a book on our desks when we arrived for work.

The book was *Dress for Success* by John Molloy, who suggested that we should dress as if we already have the job we want. I remain a believer in this advice, that your dress code should be to dress according to the job you want, not the one you have. I understand that concern with appearance is superficial compared to who we are deep down in our souls. However, it does seem reasonable to me that if you want to choose who you will be authentically, you need to know what that looks like.

I was coaching a young man in his first year at business school. Most of the students come to graduate school having worked for several years after earning their bachelor's degrees, so they arrive with some experience under their belts. Essentially, though, their entire careers are typically still in front of them. This young client was struggling with "what he really wanted to be when he grew up." He was a bit frozen on how to move forward. The issue was not whether he had options, but which was exactly the *right* option. His inertia was created by too many choices. He shared a blog post with me written by Barry Cooper called, "Beware the God of Open Options." Cooper says that we tend to want to hedge our bets. "It seems that the more options we have, the more afraid we are of choosing. We become enslaved to being noncommittal."

Cooper suggests asking such questions as "Would you prefer to make an ironclad, no-turning-back choice, or one you could back out of it need be?" and "Do you ever find that you're afraid to commit?

Going back to my client, how could he achieve clarity of direction in the face of so many options? How could he begin to narrow them? When I work with clients who are looking for new jobs or facing a decision among several alternatives, we create an exercise in which they develop filters to help eliminate some of the possibilities.

As I mentioned before, my dad was a carpenter and general handyman. I had many opportunities to watch or help him as he laid cinder blocks. To mix the mortar, he would sift the sand through a screen to eliminate larger particles that might cause the concrete to weaken over time. The size of the mesh on the screen that Dad used determined what passed through and what would be discarded. (This was before you could run to Home Depot or Lowe's and buy Ready Mix or watch a YouTube video about how to mix concrete and lay cinder blocks.) Just as my father had to determine what size screen to use for sifting, similarly, we need to evaluate our various options through the appropriate filters.

When we have choices regarding careers, we can start by making lists of what we *must* have, what we *know* we don't want, what we can live with, and so on. The best place to start in developing filters is first to decide who we want to *be*, regardless of what we *do*. What do you want family, friends, and co-workers to say when asked to describe you? It's never too early to think about the legacy you want to leave.

Examples of legacy-type descriptors are:

- Foremost expert in _____
- Great problem solver
- Deep integrity and trustworthiness
- Always reliable

- Great mentor/coach
- Inspirational speaker
- Takes initiative
- Responsible
- Talented leader

Simply put, first decide who you are going to be. Then, decide what you want to do.

Eliminate any of your options that don't support your being who you want to be. Deciding who you will be goes well beyond developing filters to help you choose opportunities. Frankly, it is essential to how you will live your life, because choosing who you will be should carry forward in every area of your life. Let me share a couple of examples.

Lee Barfield is a prominent lawyer who, in his more than forty years of practice, has tried cases in state and federal courts. He has also served numerous nonprofit organizations. When I interviewed Lee about intentional choices in his life, he wanted to share one above all others: being sober. That was no small task for him as a young man entering a university and planning a career in which he knew there would be situations involving social drinking. Lee's choice to remain a nondrinker was driven by his desire for both who he would be and who he would *not* be. Lee's mother was an alcoholic, and he witnessed firsthand the devastation of such an addiction. So, he made the decision early on not to drink. Happily, his mother eventually got into a 12-Step program and remained sober the rest of her life. I believe that his mother finally decided who she would *not* be.

At a number of business events over the years, I got to

know a bit about Kate Herman, who was once publisher of the *Nashville Business Journal*. Kate recently launched her own company, K8 Co (pronounced "Kate Co"), and I know she will continue to be successful.

Kate has long impressed me. First off, she always conducted herself in a professional manner. As I got to know her, I also found her to be smart and thoughtful, a woman with "wisdom beyond her years." Kate graciously agreed to be interviewed as part of my research for this book, and I enjoyed our conversation very much.

In particular, I was struck by one part of our discussion because of its relevancy to many discussions I have had with clients. Kate told me a story about an exercise in which she had to write her own epitaph. This caused her to stop and think, hard, about who she would be.

"So, you read these books on how to be a good manager, how to be a good leader, how to find work-life balance—how to, how to, how to," she began. "You take all this information in, which is great. I continue to read, listen to podcasts. That hasn't ended. I think what's changed is instead of me saying 'It worked for that person, so I've got to do it,' I say, 'It worked for that person, now does that work within the framework of what's important to me? How does that fit in with who I am, so that I can be the leader I want to be based on my strengths, talents, and abilities, instead of me trying to mirror other people who have done great things?'"

In conclusion, Kate added, "In doing that, I think what has happened is I'm finding great things to do on my own, rather than finding great things that other people can do that I can emulate. There's a different fulfillment and, it's almost like I'm able to accomplish more, do more, have more, contribute more to other people and what's going on because I've made that change."

Know who you are. Know who you want to be. Be that person regardless of what you do.

NON-NEGOTIABLES

Having a list of non-negotiable conditions is critical to the success of the outcome you seek. When changing jobs, what kind of work environment must you have? When choosing a life partner, what characteristics and belief systems should your mate possess? If you lead an organization, what do you consider non-negotiable with regard to the company culture? Let me give you three different illustrations of why I think this is so important.

The first business illustration comes from the interview I conducted with Craig Philip. At one point in his career, Craig was CEO of a large marine transportation company. During his tenure, there was a company-related boat traffic accident that caused him to spend a lot of time and energy understanding how such an incident might have been prevented. In that industry, company leaders have to rely on the boat captains to make their own decisions. Anytime an organization has to allow their employees such wide freedom in how they do their job, there's the challenge of orchestrating the precise balance between allowing as much autonomy as possible, yet maintaining the reputation and standards of the company. Craig realized that the company needed to establish some non-negotiable protocols and standards in order to prevent another tragic accident. Eventually, they settled on a number of requirements for maintaining safety while still affording the captains a wide range of autonomy.

A second illustration hits close to home for me personally. When my wife and I got engaged, she told me about her list of non-negotiable criteria for a husband. These were not rigid requirements about what a future husband must do; rather, they were requirements about who the future partner needed to be in terms of personality, faith, and character. After I proposed to her, she shared her list with me and told me that I met every criterion on the list. Over the years, she has shared this list with our daughter and our friends. She encourages them to make their own list before they ever get in the situation in which they may need it. We now have a teenage granddaughter who is beginning to date, and every time she talks to my wife about one of her dates, my wife reminds her that it should be non-negotiable for the boy to cherish her.

My third illustration relates to people who are either looking to change their job or career or have been asked to consider a change. When my clients are in this situation, I ask them to list what they feel must be present in the new job. The reverse of this question is also important: what must *not* be present in the new role. These questions may seem obvious or simple, but I find that considering them requires serious thought and reflection, because most people have never written those things down. Instead, we can get sidetracked by thinking that, because it sounds like a great company or the pay and benefits seem good, that will be enough. These things are certainly worth considering, but if the job opportunity does not match what you have listed as either a "must have" or a "must not have," then it likely will not be fulfilling in the long run.

What lists do you need to make in order to be true to yourself?

CHAPTER 4

Leave Your Comfort Zone

*Failure doesn't mean you are a failure, it just means
you haven't succeeded yet.*
— ROBERT H. SCHULLER

Even with their individual stories unique to their own lives,
I found common themes among the twenty-one successful
leaders I interviewed. As part of their career stories, four of
the leaders talked about critical choices they'd made regarding whether to stay in their comfort zone or make a move
into what I would label their "uncomfortable zone." I will
share brief synopses of their stories and the commonalities
among their actions. As you read, I challenge you to be open
and honest with yourself to identify your own "uncomfortable zones" such as:

- Different industry?

- A big stretch from where you are now?
- Doing something you have always wanted to do, even knowing it will be difficult?

I have known, worked with, and respected Susan Gunn for many years. I had the pleasure of observing her rapid acceleration to the highest levels of human resources within global companies. I am certain she could have secured top spots in just about any company she wanted, and that would have been both interesting and comfortable for her. But it might have been too comfortable.

In her story about choices she made, Susan told me that what had caused her to really reflect on her career was an unexpected elimination of her top-level job at a large global company.

"Your ego takes a blow, and then you have to think about what you are going to do next. What does that look like, and what do I want to do?" she said. "This is probably the first time in my life I intentionally took a step back to think very thoughtfully and carefully about what's next and what I want to do. I focused on exploration. Inasmuch as I always have a sense of urgency that I have to go on to the next big thing—keep myself relevant, be out in front of people, add value, accomplish great things—because that's what drives me and that's what gets me my juices going, I couldn't just jump into the next thing. I had done that all of my career, and this time I was going to be intentional about what I did next."

Susan realized that her career had never been intentional. When she was given opportunities, she took them and did them well. Over and over again. As her mother had taught her to do at a young age, she simply worked hard and performed at a high level. She could have continued this pattern, but she felt it was time to take a risk and be intentional about what came next. What could she do that might leverage her experience, but take her in a different direction? With the aid of assessment tools, her executive coach, and research, Susan felt she had three options.

First, she could continue doing the same type of job she'd done in the past. Maybe she would be a chief human resources officer at a public company, or a senior human resources executive at a large organization. Second, because she had more than twenty-five years of experience in great organizations across multiple geographies and cultures, she could parlay that experience to help other companies figure out and solve the problems she'd been solving for more than two decades. Third, she could move into the executive search field, as she loved pairing talent with companies and uncovering what makes people tick in various environments.

"So, I basically ran searches across all three dimensions," she said. "What was really interesting is that, as I continued that exploration, I realized I had no desire to go back to doing what I was doing in human resources." Instead, she made an intentional, bold move into human resources consulting for a large, global consulting firm. This was like nothing she had ever done before. She wouldn't have a staff, and her only vantage point at that time was as a consumer. In addition, she would be responsible for generating new business.

Susan now works for one of the largest global consulting firms, and is happy she took the intentional risk. At the time of our interview, she was relatively new to the adventure, but I have no doubt she will once again excel.

Consider another example of leaving one's comfort zone.

Janet Miller was well known for her leadership in a chamber of commerce. Because she knew that her boss would likely be in his role for many years, she knew that she either needed to look for opportunities for a top spot in other civic organizations, or do something different if she wanted to progress. Given her proven track record, it would have been both comfortable and likely that she could move to a different city and get a top role. But Janet felt it was time to get uncomfortable.

As she was going through the process of thinking about what might be possible, she was approached by a partner in a large business that was far outside of her comfort zone. The partner was impressed by her civic work, and he asked her to consider becoming CEO of one region of an international real estate services and investment company that was made up mostly of male leaders. Other factors in her "discomfort zone" included: being a CEO in a company that historically made decisions through consensus, though they often had trouble agreeing; having little knowledge of the industry; knowing that, because she'd be one of only two females at the table for parent company meetings, being seen and heard might be a challenge; and needing to win over team members in an industry where they all work largely independently.

Janet decided it was now or never. She hired an executive coach to help her make the transformation to the person she needed to be in the new role. Recently, Janet was named a partner in the parent company. She has moved from discomfort to success.

Some people build their lives and careers moving from discomfort zone to discomfort zone. John Ferguson is a great example. He started his career with IBM. From there, his career had many twists and turns, each taking him out of his current comfort zone. He went from starting a used computer company to helping launch an inner city ministry for at-risk youth; from banking to public service in state government; and back to private business as CEO of a prison management firm.

In another chapter, I addressed the choice to be authentic in whatever you do even though you may need to *be* different in different roles. Because John had so many vastly different roles, I asked him if he had needed to change who he was being, depending on which job he had. For example, moving from private business to a nonprofit organization or public service were pretty significant shifts. I asked John, "Did you have to be somebody different?"

"Probably not," he replied. "I developed some organizational skills and some management skills along the way . . . . Now that you asked that question, though, obviously the outcomes were different. But I probably approached the outcomes a little differently than maybe somebody who'd always been in the nonprofit or government sectors."

John went back to private business after finding a successor at the nonprofit, but in another interesting twist, he was asked to serve in a governor's administration. "So that, again, was a behavioral change. I had to adapt my style and learn how to be effective in the ways that government works."

Cordia Harrington is founder and CEO of the Bakery Companies. In October 2020, she made *Forbes* magazine's list of 100 Richest Self-Made Women. In 2018, she'd been inducted into the American Society of Baking Hall of Fame, and she is recognized nationally as one of the most influential and successful women in her industry. Cordia is a confident person, full of internal drive. Early on, she moved from being a single mom to working in real estate. Then she became one of the first women to own a McDonald's franchise. Later, she owned her own company, which in turn became a supplier to her former food services brand. So, what in the world would make a person that successful uncomfortable? Giving up some of the control of her business.

Cordia's business was successful, but she knew it could be even better. She belonged to a CEO peer group that served as accountability partners for each other. Cordia built her business, in part, based on instinct and tenacity, but it was a bit of a shock to her when one member of her peer group said, "Instinct is not scalable."

A trusted advisor gave her the tough advice that she should instead hire a CEO familiar with the industry and focus her own attention on new ways to expand her business. With some reluctance, she hired the CEO, but the transition to letting go of day-to-day control—and staying out of certain decisions—was not easy. Over time, she and the new CEO developed an agreement around how they would know when she was stepping back into areas she had handed over to him. They agreed that, when she was overstepping her bounds, he would say the word "boot." When he said that word, she knew it was time to turn around and walk out of his office and let him run the business. They purchased a boot and put it in the corner of his office. Anytime she crossed the line, he would point at the boot to indicate that he could handle the matter at hand. At the time of this significant change, the company was at about $20 million in revenue. As of 2020, it had grown to more than $200 million.

Perhaps you're thinking, if it's her company, why can't she overstep her bounds anytime she wants? To some extent, that might be true, but she and the CEO had agreed that the boundaries they set were important to the ultimate success of the parent company.

Let's look at commonalities among these stories. All these leaders:

- Understood themselves and appreciated their transferrable skills
- Had confidence in their abilities to adapt
- Committed to stretch themselves beyond their comfort zones
- Built reputations for getting things done
- Reached out to trusted advisors (peers, executive coaches, friends, family)
- Trusted that, even if the leap did not turn out as expected, at least they would grow
- Developed accountability partners, often their trusted advisors
- Surrounded themselves with knowledgeable people

Now that I have shared some of the stories of leaders who intentionally left their comfort zones and lived to tell about it, let's examine what tends to hold us back from challenging ourselves.

What Holds You Back?

For one thing, we're afraid of failure. In our success-driven culture, no one wants to fail. Yet we all do, at one time or another, in one way or another. Maybe you make a minor misstep, or perhaps your action has long-term negative implications. It's part of life. I've mentioned a friend's approach of "failing forward." You can always learn something. And if you're failing, at least you're trying.

We're also scared of letting go of what we have, being vulnerable in new situations, and leaving our comfort zones. Some of this fear comes from not knowing ourselves well enough. We don't acknowledge our inner strengths, perhaps, or we dismiss the potential others see in us.

Another reason we might not challenge ourselves includes not recognizing the cost of staying put. Later, there could be long-term regrets about what might have been. And often we don't plan far enough ahead. Waiting too long to make a decision can result in the disappearance of the opportunity. We need to make an honest and thorough inventory of what will be required of us to make a change.

Carolyn Freer-Jones found herself in a position in which a whole new world of possibilities existed in front of her. But transitioning to this new world brought up a fear of failure. Carolyn chose to do something radical, something that required a major shift in mindset. She said that her journey into her own business was both terrifying and wildly exciting. As she weighed the pros and cons of starting her own business, a key factor in her ultimate decision was the fear of missing out if she didn't try.

Many times, I have seen people focus on the possible downsides of a certain action, all the while ignoring the risks associated with *not* choosing to do something. I like to think of this as the "lost opportunity" cost. Typically, new coaching engagements start with a complimentary coaching session. If someone is undecided about whether to proceed with coaching, I often ask, "What will happen if you don't do coaching?" If they don't think they'd be missing anything, then I usually recommend they not do coaching.

John Deane had a successful career in healthcare, including starting his own company, growing it, and merging with a much larger company. Most entrepreneurs I know struggle with being part of a bigger organization after they sell their companies. This was true for John as well, and he wondered what to do next. Knowing when "enough is enough" is difficult, but important on several levels such as financial, career, and personal. You'll need to decide for yourself how much money you need, how many titles or promotions you desire, and what matters most in your personal life. Only you can determine when "enough is enough."

John decided that, from both a career and financial standpoint, he'd had enough. He retired from the healthcare industry earlier than some. The central theme running through John's decision-making all along was the realization that taking good care of himself, and taking time for himself, would be important in whatever he did next. After the decision to retire, John and his wife set up a nonprofit organization to foster civic engagement. He also found that, with the extra time, he could pursue a business investment for which he was passionate.

Previously, I talked about the choice to leave your comfort zone and go in an entirely different direction. But many people are faced with a different but equally difficult choice. They reach a point in their career where they start to wonder what the highest and best use of the remainder of their career might look like.

Jerry Hickson was a practicing pediatrician who became interested in academics. He pursued teaching and research at a prominent university. He was approached by the university's chief medical officer about leading an important initiative that would require him to work across all medical disciplines rather than continue to specialize in pediatrics.

Jerry was asked to lead a team to study physician behavior and its relationship to incidences of malpractice lawsuits, and to develop an approach to help physicians choose to self-modify negative behaviors. In my experience as an executive coach, getting people to acknowledge—and make—necessary behavioral shifts can be difficult, especially when they've been successful in some respects using their current behaviors.

Jerry had a choice to make. He could continue to pursue research and teaching in pediatrics, which would be rewarding, or take a path with many unknowns—including the real impact he might have. It was a time of serious reflection about which path would represent the highest and best use of his values, training, experience, and desires. He chose to accept the challenge and lead the new team.

Financial Realities

Let's be realistic. There are times in our lives in which obligations may demand that we remain right where we are for the foreseeable future. If this is where you find yourself, here are possible strategies to get yourself in a different position:

- Develop strong financial strategies (Dave Ramsey's Financial Peace University is one resource for this, and there are many others)
- Revisit your dream when your situation allows for more freedom—maybe when your children are out on their own, or your obligations to others have decreased
- Plan now for what it will take to achieve your dream in the future

These stories might not match your exact situation, but I hope something resonates. Maybe you have reached a plateau in your career. Maybe you are stuck deciding what is next for you. Maybe there is a dream to chase.

What holds you back?

CHANGING DIRECTION

Sometimes what we are called to do is almost the polar opposite of what we think. A case in point is a former client who was making a dramatic change in order to pursue a passion she'd had for many years. Thanks to her career success, she'd reached a point where she could step aside and chase her dream.

As we worked together, it became clear that there was a certain direction in which she did not want to go. She did her due diligence, including writing in her journal about what she wanted, and pursuing connections that would help her to make it happen. However, in the course of her research and exploration, everything seemed to lead her toward the very thing she said she did not want to do, and away from the direction she originally thought would be right for her. But she paid attention and considered her options. Wonderfully, she is now passionate about serving and helping in the area that was of least interest to her when she started.

CHAPTER 5

Shift Behavior

I am not a product of my circumstances. I am a product of my decisions.

—STEPHEN R. COVEY

I'm sure you're familiar with the saying, "A leopard can't change its spots." Typically, that phrase is used when we don't want to change a bad behavior. Through my work as a coach, I would modify the statement to say, "A leopard can't change its spots unless the leopard wants to change its spots." Changing spots is not easy, but it can be done. I have witnessed "leopards" who, through intentional and committed choices, did indeed change their spots.

Take Eddie Hutton, a man I believe was born to be an entrepreneur. Over the course of his career he bought a small air conditioning company, which he ultimately took public. At the same time, he was working in commercial real estate development. Anytime I ask Eddie how he's doing, his response is always "better than I deserve," and he truly believes that. He attributes his success to be a gift from God. One of the things I like about Eddie is that from this recognition flows a passion to use his success to benefit others. In particular, he has a strong passion for working with men in prison.

At one point in his life, Eddie had been an excellent golfer. He loved the game, and he even went to college on a golf scholarship. After graduation, he spent all of his spare time on the golf course. In 2002, then in his mid-forties, he had a heart attack. It proved to be a wake-up call.

As Eddie reflected on his state of mind back then, he realized that staying on his trajectory of spending all his time on the golf course would not encourage a healthy lifestyle, thereby denying him time with his family. That was time he didn't want to squander. Eddie had to make a difficult choice. He knew other people who were passionate about a sport and yet maintained the proper balance. But he felt that his best course of action was to choose between the sport and who he wanted to be. He gave up golf and the country club scene in order to spend quality time with his family and friends. Many years later, he has no regrets about the choice. Occasionally, he feels the "call of the game," and he has learned that he can play when he wants without falling back into his previous all-consuming pattern.

Around the same time Eddie was making his decision about golf, he also realized he needed to let go of some of his control of the businesses he operated. So he did.

None of these choices were easy, but he was committed to them. That kind of commitment sometimes leads to failures, and Eddie used those failures as opportunities for personal growth. When I asked Eddie about holding himself accountable to his commitments, he said he was primarily accountable to himself, and to God.

I haven't had a heart attack, but I did undergo open heart surgery. Something like that certainly brings you face to face with the recognition that life is fleeting, and that every day is a gift. I suspect that many of you reading this book have had some life-altering moments of your own.

I absolutely believe we are each uniquely created and gifted by our Creator, but that our behaviors are also influenced by experiences we have, habits we learn, stories we've created about ourselves, and stories we adopt from what others say about us. I am also a firm believer in using assessment tools to learn more about ourselves, but I caution you against limiting yourself in response to whatever "labels"— or even "spots"—such tests might suggest.

For example, just because a test shows you have tendencies toward introversion—which simply suggests you get more enjoyment and energy from an inner life—that doesn't mean you're without extroverted qualities. Whatever you do, don't allow the categories to hold you back. Some of the most successful salespeople I know, people you might automatically assume to be extroverts (people who get more enjoyment and energy from being around others), would describe themselves as introverted. The successful sales introverts I have known have found a way to call up the energy they need in particular situations and developed ways to recharge after the draining situations are behind them.

Regardless of personality type, we will all have times in our lives and our work that require us to do some things that are unpleasant or tiring. This just comes with life. However, it is important to know what does give us energy so that we can find ways to recharge our batteries as we deal with tedious activities. Stop for a minute and think about what gives you energy. Make a list and keep it where you can easily access it.

You probably have known some people who came across as confident and outgoing in front of an audience, but who are actually shy and reserved when not on the stage. I often find that people hide behind a label to excuse some of their behaviors.

For example, I've had several clients who often offended others but excused their own behavior by saying, "I am just very direct." Others have said, "I could never speak up in a group because I'm an introvert." Hiding behind a label can prevent you from doing the hard work of spot removal.

Where are you limiting yourself by hiding behind a label?

Recently, I had an interesting conversation with a man who works in leadership development with individuals. Although he was not a client of mine, the purpose of our conversation was to share the results of an assessment tool I had administered for him. I wanted to illustrate the use of this tool as a potential aid for him with his own clients. There were a couple of things in the assessment that surprised me a bit about him, relative to my personal assessment of him based on his background and a prior conversation. I asked him to tell me about what he thought was driving this particular score. Much to my surprise, he considered the score accurate and admitted he had a few struggles that weren't evident to people he encountered in his work. The moral of that story, for me, is never accept what is on the surface, but instead ask questions that require deeper thought. Just the fact that he and I had this conversation led him to conclude that there were a few areas in his life where he needed to let go of what others think.

CHANGE WHO YOU ARE BEING, NOT WHO YOU ARE

How do you remain authentic while changing your spots?

Sometimes, clients who have made comments that are deemed offensive are referred to me by their human resources departments as a condition of their continued employment. Without exception, in our initial conversation the new client offers some version of: "I am just direct, and I call them as I see them. I don't understand why that is a problem. More people should be like me."

As a guiding principle, it would, indeed, prevent a lot of thorny issues if more people used straightforward communication. In fact, one of the core competencies for executive coaches is "direct communication." So, what is the problem my clients have faced? The issue always centers around style of delivery and choice of words. The tone of your voice, your body language, and the words you choose make all the difference in how your message is received. Some examples of ineffective communication are:

- Asking questions that begin with "why," as in: "Why did you do____?"
- Delivering any message when you are angry
- Sending an email when you are upset
- Using offensive language when making a point
- Sharing a thought when it is not helpful or requested

If you are direct by nature, but want to be more effective and less offensive in your communication, here are some tips:

- Get feedback from people you trust on how they view your directness. Are there times they've found it effective? Offensive?
- Observe yourself in various situations and note how you are received. What was happening within you when the communication was effective, and when it was not?
- Read *Crucial Conversations: Tools for Talking When Stakes Are High*, by Kerry Patterson and Joseph Grenny, et al. and read it again every several years
- Identify the behavior you want to change
- Invite a few people you trust, such as your new accountability partners, to observe you, and give them permission to let you know when you're missing the mark

We all have habits that give others an impression about us that is either positive or negative, although we may not be aware of such habits. In the greater scheme of things, these behaviors may not seem important, but in reality, they are part of the total person we project to others.

Now, let's talk about an example of changing who you are *being* without changing who you *are*. Earlier, I mentioned Janet Miller—CEO of a regional office of a global real estate development firm. Today her industry continues to be dominated by men, especially in the top leadership roles. When she stepped out of her comfort zone and took on her current position, Janet realized that, to be successful, she needed to be heard when she sat at the leadership table. She knew she had to speak with authority. With the help of her coach, she developed a strong picture of what it would look like to speak with authority. In my interview with her, she told me that to prepare for those meetings she would remind herself that she could be heard by being a certain way. With this vision in mind, she would say to herself, "Bring *that* girl" when going into a situation where she needed to speak with authority.

I believe we can be who we need to be (or, our authentic selves) even in different situations that require varying actions and responses. Janet's vision of "that girl" included being:

- Prepared: Doing more pre-meeting prep than most people would do
- Confident: Relying on past successes to generate confidence
- Assertive: Knowing when to speak up, and not hesitating to do so
- Authoritative: Speaking with authority
- Herself: At her core, Janet is respectful, kind, considerate, smart, and full of sound ideas

Your version of "that girl" or "that guy" will need to be tailored to your personality, your objectives, and your environment. Remember to let your authenticity guide you, and be sure to trust your foundational qualities, regardless of what situation you find yourself in.

Who do you need to be?

CHAPTER 6

Change Habits

Excellence is an art won by training and habituation.
—ARISTOTLE

This book was finalized during the global COVID-19 pandemic. The sudden "stay at home/work from home" requirements were a major disruption of habits. To be sure, many of my coaching clients struggled with the loss of routine in their daily lives. Without boundaries imposed by such routines as getting to the office and returning home at certain times, clients found they were available—or presumed to be—24/7.

How did the loss of routines disrupt your habits during the pandemic? Did you learn new boundaries and develop new habits? How did you adapt? Did you develop new habits you can take forward in your life?

Some clients began taking walks during what would

have been their commute time, so as to feel as if they were "leaving for work." This helped them shift their mindset, even though they were working from home. Another client got in her car each morning and drove to her office's parking lot, then turned around and came back home as a way to signal the start of her workday.

There is a considerable body of work surrounding habits, and I only skim the surface here. I have not conducted formal research or testing on this topic, but I draw from my own experiences and those of my clients. In fact, much within our everyday lives is based on a large stack of habits.

To illustrate the point, just think about your day so far. How many things did you do today that were, essentially, automated activities requiring no serious thought? You have done them so many times that you don't even have to think about it. It could be as simple as a pattern you tend to follow from when you get up in the morning until you leave for work or start your plans for the day. We all develop habits that become automatic.

In his book *The Power of Habit*, Charles Duhigg looks at various aspects of life such as cravings, coaching, and leadership. He connects them to, essentially, the same cycle of cue, routine (response), and reward.

"This process within our brains is a three-step loop," says Duhigg. "First, there is a cue, a trigger that tells your brain to go into automatic mode and which habit to use. Then there is the routine, which can be physical or mental or emotional. Finally, there is a reward, which helps your brain figure out if this particular loop is worth remembering for the future . . . . Over time, this loop—cue, routine, reward; cue, routine, reward—becomes more and more automatic. . . ."

I suspect that, because I took a course in electrical engineering while working on my undergraduate degree in industrial engineering, I think of habits as wiring a circuit or switch. If you want to change a habit, you'll need to rewire the circuit in order to get a different outcome. All of us have learned a response or two over time that becomes almost automatic when triggered. In coaching, this comes out frequently when discussing how we react to certain people or circumstances.

Understanding how habits work is key to changing them. If you have certain responses or habits that need your attention, consider developing a reward system to incentivize your efforts. For example, one client lives in a large city and within walking access to an Italian ice shop nearby. She decided to start thinking of going to the shop as a reward when she had completed an important project or survived a long, demanding day. She said that just the act of reframing how she thought about the shop made the experience more rewarding.

I have heard numerous suggestions about how long it takes to change a habit or behavior. Some sources say fourteen days, while others suggest twenty-one days or more. You might have heard a different number. I think it depends on the complexity of what you are trying to change and the frequency with which you have an opportunity to practice.

At one time, I had a client who would frequently apologize for having an opinion. Actually, she would apologize several times in one conversation. We worked on that tendency, and eventually she was able to stop herself before apologizing unnecessarily.

I have seen people make a significant shift in behavior like this over a two- to three-week period. But your situation may take longer to resolve. There is no one-size-fits-all in terms of timeframe. However, I have found a fairly simple approach to changing behavior. The change itself may not be easy, but the process is straightforward.

I like to think about changing a habit as a process. While tweaks may be necessary depending on the habit, the process works in the same way, conceptually, as Duhigg's "cue, routine, reward":

- First, observe yourself a few times to note the circumstances when you're triggered
- Example: you're usually tired, or it's always the same personality type
- Now, observe yourself a few more times, paying attention to what you are feeling physically at the split second the response is triggered
- Example: you feel your body grow tense
- Note what happens the second your response is triggered and how others react
- Create alternative responses with different outcomes/ rewards
- Test the new approach, adjust if necessary, and keep practicing
- Observe the impact of the new response
- Celebrate your success

Sometimes, we develop habits without being aware of how we come across to others. I remember two different occasions in which people pointed out habits of mine that made them feel I was not confident as their leader. In one instance, someone pointed out that I had a bad habit of rubbing my hands together when I talked about a difficult problem. They said I appeared worried, and that made them question whether I knew what I was doing. The second occurred while traveling with a business associate. We were walking along, when all of a sudden she said, "Stand up straight, because you look like a question mark and it makes you seem like you are carrying the weight of the world on your shoulders, which is very distracting." On the surface, it seemed both of my bad habits were so trivial and automatic that I did not even notice, but clearly others did. In both cases, I made it a point to catch myself before exhibiting one of these behaviors, and to switch to a new habit. I cannot tell you that I am always successful, but I *can* tell you the unwelcome behaviors occur less frequently.

What habits do you need to change?

CHANGING HABITS

In title, my client was at the level of senior management in her organization. But in reality, she felt she was continuing to do administrative rather than management level functions. Her leadership felt it would be good for her to work with a coach to help her be the senior leader she aspired to be.

We had to address some of the things that were holding her back from becoming who she wanted to be. One of those things was a habit of apologizing frequently when sharing her ideas, views, and reasonings. I found it distracting during calls with her, and asked if she'd ever had feedback from others about this. She said that her husband often told her he wished she would stop apologizing so frequently. The thing to note here is that, although this might seem like harmless behavior, it led other people to believe she lacked confidence.

We approached shifting her behavior by essentially following the process described in my Change Habits chapter. We began by having her simply observe herself for a couple weeks, and be specially attuned to how frequently she apologized. The other approach we used was to have both her husband and me point out when she was apologizing, and challenge her to find a different way to state her view without apology. When we start closely observing our behavior, we become hypersensitive to the onset of our actions. My client became instinctively aware of her frequency of apologizing, and thus began recognizing the moment she was about to apologize. At that point, she began to practice stopping herself. She was successful in choosing a different behavior, which then resulted in others noticing her increased confidence when she spoke.

CHAPTER 7

Broaden Perspectives

No man will make a great leader who wants to do it all himself, or to get all the credit for doing it.
—ANDREW CARNEGIE

The dictionary has a number of different meanings for the word "perspective," depending on how it is being used. One definition is "the state of one's ideas, the facts known to one." In other words, perspective is how you choose to look at things, given what you already know. As an artist and a recovering engineer, it takes on a bit of a different meaning for me. I had to learn to see objects from many different angles before I could understand how to draw or paint them.

When I was painting a bench on a cliff that looked toward the ocean in Laguna Beach, California, I had to decide what perspective I wanted for the scene. Up close, I noticed the details of the bench and a few of the flowers that surrounded it. From the next cliff, looking back toward the area, I could see the bench, the ocean in front of it, the distant hills, and an abundance of flowers, plants, and beautiful scenery. Taking a different perspective opened a whole new world of possibilities.

In his book, *The Simple Secret to Better Painting: How to Immediately Improve Your Art with the One Rule of Composition*, Greg Albert has some interesting thoughts about perspective. "Perspective used well will give your pictures a convincing sense of depth and enhance the believability," he says. "Perspective can also be used to enhance the composition of your paintings."

Although Albert was specifically talking about art, it struck me that, with a bit of paraphrasing, these statements also have application for leadership. How might your leadership be more effective if you seek others' perspectives as you develop your visions and goals? Consider that seeking a number of perspectives will give your visions and goals a convincing sense of depth, and enhance their believability. Different perspectives can also be used to enhance the composition of your vision.

When I coach clients—and sometimes even in casual conversations with friends—I'm always delighted when something I say causes them to respond with, "I never thought about it quite like that." To me, it is an indication that new possibilities are now open for them. And they can be open for you, too.

Let's look at a couple of examples of considering new perspectives from one successful leader. Darrell Freeman grew up in a loving family, but his parents never finished high school. He was the first in his family to go to college.

Despite their lack of formal education, his parents had the wisdom that one needs for life. In many ways, Darrell's story reminds me of my own. His father saw life from the perspective of his thirty-eight years of working in a foundry, and he had a different idea about what he wanted for Darrell. You may recall that my dad said he wanted me to be a "pencil pusher," and not a manual laborer like him. Darrell's dad told him to have a job where you "shower in the morning rather than at night." And Darrell's mother was definitely one who focused on what was possible.

Darrell told me that, when he was growing up, he would often look in the refrigerator and see very little to eat, but his mother could see a delicious meal. I have thought of this often since I sat down with Darrell for our interview. I would challenge you to be like Darrell's mother. When you are in a situation in which all of the ingredients don't seem to be there, pause and ask yourself, "What might I make with the ingredients on hand?" Change your perspective.

This is often true in business as well. If we limit our perspective, we may not see the bigger picture or grander possibilities. As leaders, we need to be skilled at looking at situations from many different angles. For example, I have seen many specialized salespeople interact with clients in what I describe as a "transaction mode." The idea is that *you* have a specific need, and *I* offer a specific solution for that need. Cut and dry, if you will. However, people who want to provide the highest level of service start by first understanding their clients' overall goals.

As part of my job at the time, I spent more than ten years interviewing a financial services firm's clients, asking them about their goals and what mattered to them. A theme I heard across a wide spectrum of clients, from small to global organizations was, "I want you to really understand our business and our company goals, and then bring us solutions and products that help us achieve those goals."

When you understand the bigger picture of the client's goals and directions, you start to develop a true partnership. As leaders, it is dangerous to assume that we intuitively know what is best for our clients, our associates, and even our families. For any given situation, there are a number of affected parties, all of whom have a legitimate viewpoint. Gather all the perspectives you can.

I can't overstate the power that considering additional perspectives can have on your ability to lead. Many of my clients have reported that looking at something from multiple angles has been nothing short of transformative for their professional and personal lives.

Circling back to my interview with Darrell Freeman, he told me that he'd attempted to go to college a couple of times, but limited finances and lack of effort on his part made him think he would end up in the foundry like his father. Then, a friend asked Darrell to help him move into a university dorm. When he saw that his friend had "his own room, his own phone, and a meal plan where he could eat every day," he said, "I have got to go to school here." That experience opened a whole new world of possibilities for Darrell, and he went on to start a technology company while still in college. So, not only did he decide to be successful in school, but he also decided to be successful in life. Eventually, he would cofound a bank. Today he serves on a number of nonprofit boards, and uses the resources provided by his success to help others understand what is possible for them with an education.

Jane (not her real name) is another example of applying passion to different areas of one's life. For many years, Jane was a successful dancer on Broadway and director for a number of plays in New York, before transitioning to a career in financial services. After a big promotion, she needed to change who she was being in order to be successful. In her new role, she would inherit an existing team of people, and she needed to be sure the right players were in the right place and that everyone knew their respective roles and executed them effectively.

One day, while we talked about past work roles that had energized her, she mentioned her time as a play director. She said that she was always invigorated when making sure all the actors were at their proper spots on the stage and understood the rules. I asked her how she could apply the skills it took to successfully direct a play to her current work situation. She realized that, even with a different title, her new role had a lot in common with being a director. To mark this insight, she found a small toy director's chair and put it on her desk as a reminder of how to bring forward her proven skills into an entirely different situation.

Think about a business decision you need to make, or a solution you need to develop. Before you move forward, talk to someone who may be affected by the decision and ask for his or her input. If you really want to have fun, ask several people. Then ask yourself if getting these perspectives changed your decision or alerted you to considerations that you had overlooked. If the answer is yes, then add this best practice to your leadership toolkit. If the answer is no, ask yourself if you were really listening. Remember, your own perspective will only get you so far.

Where do you need to broaden your perspective?

CHAPTER 8

Mind Your Brain

The biggest benefit that positive thoughts provide is an enhanced ability to build skills and develop resources for use later in life.
—BARBARA FREDERICKSON

A book on the power of choice would be incomplete without a discussion of how your brain impacts your ability to make and accomplish transformational choices. As you might imagine, the relevant research runs the gamut. Some of what I uncovered while writing *The Art of Choice* is densely scientific. Because I do not intend for this chapter, or this book, to be an academic treatment of the neuroscience behind the art of making decisions, I don't include a lot of it here and instead focus on what I consider to be more accessible information.

If you would like to know more about brain research, there are many articles and books on the topic. (Please see

Recommended Resources for a few suggestions.) My discussion here incorporates what I've learned with what I've seen work for my coaching clients. I've also benefitted from adopting these same strategies myself. My hope is that this chapter will provide you with new perspectives, broaden your thinking, and offer tools for helping you accomplish the choices you make.

I am not sure when all the research around what happens in the brain regarding choices began, but I know that the topic got considerable attention with the 1952 publication of *The Power of Positive Thinking* by Norman Vincent Peale. I have found Peale's work to be instrumental in how I make my way in the world.

While going through life and building my career, I'm not sure I always considered how my thinking influenced my success or lack thereof. I suspect that most people who know me would tell you I am generally upbeat and positive, but I'm not sure I necessarily understood how to connect positive thoughts to the outcome I wanted when I was younger. I do now, and it's made a world of difference for me both personally and professionally.

I have come to believe that how you *choose* to think plays a major role in whether or not you accomplish the changes you want to make. I understand there may be external circumstances that interfere with your success, but how you choose to think is up to you. And I suggest that being curious about how your brain works can help you make strides in making sound choices.

Christopher Bergland—endurance athlete, coach, author, and public health advocate—says, "Decision-making is in the locus of your control. You have the power to break patterns of behavior simply by making better decisions. You can change your mind and your actions at any time." I agree wholeheartedly with Bergland.

Once, during a conversation with my own executive coach, he asked, "Is the problem the problem, or is how you *think* about the problem the problem?" At first, I was taken aback by this question, but as I thought about it more, I realized that indeed it was how I was *thinking* about the problem that was creating the real problem. I changed my thinking and found a solution.

There are many approaches that can assist you in changing your thinking and thereby redirecting your future. As for me and my clients, we have benefitted from trying to better understand how our brains work, by shifting to positive thinking as our main way of being in the world, and by engaging in mindfulness. Maybe some of these can help you, too.

As Norman Vincent Peale began talking and writing about positive thinking, he quickly gained both supporters and critics. Critics homed in on his lack of scientific research, and pointed out that some of Peale's conclusions were opinion, not fact. Regardless, as the body of research grew around the topic, the broad idea that positive thinking directly impacts positive outcomes has been validated many times. I claim no scientific training or credentials around this topic, but as a lifelong observer of myself and others, and through my work as an executive coach, I have no doubts about how positive thinking supports positive outcomes. Here are a couple of quotes from Norman Vincent Peale that speak to me:

- "Believe in yourself! Have faith in your abilities! Without a humble but reasonable confidence in your

own powers you cannot be successful or happy."
- "Even people who have a long record of NOT succeeding can be turned into tremendous achievers if they will discard their images of themselves as failures."

There is solid science to support the power of positive thinking. According to an article in *The Atlantic*, "...hundreds of academic papers have been published studying the health effects of expecting good things to happen, which researchers call 'dispositional optimism.' They've linked this positive outlook on life to everything from decreased feelings of loneliness to increased pain tolerance."

In her book, *Insight: The Surprising Truth About How Others See Us, How We See Ourselves, and Why the Answers Matter More Than We Think*, organizational psychologist Tasha Eurich provides one simple but important example of how positive or negative thoughts can have an impact on the options we see as being available to us. "...*Why* questions draw us to our limitations; *what* questions help us see our potential. *Why* questions stir up negative emotions; *what* questions keep us curious. *Why* questions trap us in our past; *what* questions help us create a better future."

Barbara Fredrickson, researcher and Distinguished Professor of Psychology at the University of North Carolina, has great insights on the power of positive thinking, a few of which I summarize here:

- Negative emotions narrow your mind and focus your thoughts
- Positive emotions broaden your sense of possibility and open your mind to more options

- Positive thought provides an enhanced ability to build skills and develop resources for use later in life

The way I like to think about all of this is to realize that negative thoughts drain your energy, and positive thoughts *give* you energy.

What thoughts give you energy? What thoughts drain your energy?

I have not scratched the surface of the work that has been done around positive thinking, or the neuroscience behind making choices, or mindfulness, but I wanted to share what all of this says to me. You can limit or expand the possibilities open to you by how you choose to think. In his letter to the Philippians, the apostle Paul said it well:

> Summing it all up friends, I'd say you'll do best
> by filling your minds and meditating on things
> true, noble, reputable, authentic, compelling,
> gracious—the best not the worst; the beautiful,
> not the ugly; things of praise,
> not things to curse.
> —PHILIPPIANS 4:8 (*THE MESSAGE*)

Mindfulness

I find Eurich's definition of mindfulness to be simple and clear. "Mindfulness is simply noticing what we're thinking, feeling, and doing without judgment or reaction." I also like how Ellen Langer, who became the first tenured female professor in psychology at Harvard, described mindfulness in Eurich's book as "the process of actively noticing new things, relinquishing preconceived mindsets, and then acting on . . . [our] new observations." While others may define mindfulness differently, I prefer the broad, accessible language of Eurich and Langer. As a coach, I think of it in part as being completely present in the moment.

According to the Dana Foundation, a private philanthropic organization dedicated to advancing understanding about the brain, "From a neuroscience perspective, the attraction to apply mindfulness to education stems from how the practice changes the brain. Meditation seems to particularly influence two major brain systems: attention and emotion. Greater self-regulation of these systems enables focused attention without distraction and the capacity to exercise control over emotional impulses."

Mindfulness is about being present in the moment. Freeing oneself from distracting thoughts regarding the past or the future, and being fully focused on the here and now. Here is one simple exercise that works well for me and many of my clients:

- Sit upright in a chair, feet flat on the floor, arms at rest
- Take a deep breath
- Focus your mind only on your feet, while breathing in and out slowly
- Next, focus your mind on the weight of your body on the seat of the chair, and continue breathing slowly
- Change focus and repeat next with your arms, then your head
- Finally, focus completely on the breath coming in and out of your nose
- Notice how you feel now, versus how you felt when you started

Years ago, I was on a conference call with mindfulness expert Doug Silsbee when he asked all participants to do the exercise above. My first reaction was "this is nuts," but I decided I would go along for the ride. When we finished the exercise, I was shocked to find I was much more relaxed.

If you study mindfulness, you will most likely learn other ways to approach it. But I find this simple act to be very effective when I am really stressed, or going into what I know may be a difficult conversation, or even right before a coaching session. Taking a few minutes to center myself makes a great difference.

You might consider an app such as Calm or Breathe (there are many to choose from), or make a "stop" sign and tape it to your phone as a reminder to take a breath before a difficult call.

Practical Tools to Increase Positive Thought

From my research and my observations over time, creating positive thoughts and feelings does indeed open your mind to greater possibilities. I have no magic formula, but here are a few ways that have worked for either myself or others. However you approach generating positive thoughts, be intentional.

Meditation

I like to keep things simple, so this dictionary.com definition suits me: "Meditation is continued or extended thought; reflection; contemplation." For me, the straightforward definition makes the topic accessible to everyone. How one approaches achieving extended thought, reflection, and so on is, of course, different for each individual; but what is important is the effectiveness that meditation has on generating positive thoughts.

I have mentioned before that I believe the Bible is the best management book I know, and of course it has something to say about meditation.

> This Book of the Law shall not depart from
> your mouth, but you shall meditate on it day
> and night, so that you may be careful to do
> according to all that is written in it. For then you
> will make your way prosperous, and then you
> will have good success.
> —JOSHUA 1:8 (NIV)

How do you proactively create time and space for reflection and contemplation? Perhaps you take walks in nature, practice yoga, or find a quiet spot in your home. Most of the time, my meditation is the quiet time that I spend with a devotional and my Bible early in the morning, but sometimes it is a stroll along the beach or through a neighborhood.

For many years, my wife and I rented a house near a pond on Cape Cod. Spending my early morning quiet times in the Adirondack chairs by the pond was like being plugged into a recharging station. Know what serves as a recharging station for you, and make time to plug in—whether your station comes in the form of simply being in a place, or doing morning or evening devotionals, meditation, yoga, or exercise.

I experienced some of the best moments of reflection and contemplation sitting in those chairs watching the sun come up. It is my happy place, and parts of this book were written from those chairs.

Where is your happy place? Put down this book and think about it. If you don't have one, I suggest you get busy in determining where just such a spot might be for you. Take yourself there in your mind when you need to calm or inspire yourself.

While in many respects, meditation and mindfulness may be achieved in similar ways (breathing, focusing, and so on), some people prefer to engage in reflection and contemplation while moving. Try exploring a nature preserve, strolling in your neighborhood (without your phone!), or walking a labyrinth.

Writing

Every morning, my wife writes in her journal. Maybe she recalls what happened the day before, or perhaps she anticipates the day ahead. She also often goes back and reads what she wrote on the same day the year before. Sometimes, the journal entry is long and contemplative, and other days it is mostly a recording of key events, people, and places. Whether my wife writes two sentences or two pages, journaling calms and centers her, which, in turn, leads to more positive thinking.

I don't enjoy journaling, so it is not one of my go-to practices. But I have learned that writing things down is a major first step for anything important. For example, in a coaching session with a CEO being groomed for a bigger role in the parent company, he told me that his chairman instructed him to learn more about areas of the company where he had little knowledge. My client had been doing this somewhat casually. But, as we talked, he realized he needed to make a list of specific areas in which he needed to be intentional in his approach to learning. The simple act of writing down such tasks will bring focus.

What does making a list have to do with positive thinking or neuroscience? It is really quite simple: the process of writing causes the mind to feel better, because there is more clarity.

Play

Regardless of what "play" looks like for you, it likely brings fun, happy thoughts, stress relief, and hopefully better health all around. I am a professional artist, but for me, painting is still like play. It is a mental escape.

One of our sons has always loved playing baseball, and as an adult he continues to play in softball leagues. We have never had an official conversation about that pursuit being a joy to him, but I can sense his passion even when we are simply discussing how his team is doing. It is truly restorative for him.

I had one young client who was going through a period of extreme stress and self-doubt. I actually became a bit concerned about him. He made an intentional plan to go to an ice rink one night because, in the past, playing hockey helped him clear his mind, relieve stress, and open up options for ways to deal with whatever he was facing.

THE BOTTOM LINE

You may be wondering why I have devoted so many pages to talking about the importance of how your thinking can influence your choices and outcomes. Because it is that important.

Circling back and paraphrasing what my coach asked

me, I am asking you to consider where in your life how you *think* about a problem is actually the real problem.

The ability to shift your perspective and broaden your options is already within you. You can choose whether to have positive thoughts and see more options or be negative and limit your options. From a practical standpoint, the examples I have shared and the many others I have witnessed are all I need to absolutely know anyone can make transformational choices and be successful. But my belief is also supported by neuroscience. Choice is in the locus of your control. You have the power to break patterns of behavior simply by making better choices. You can change your mind and your actions at any time.

How might you adjust your thinking toward more positive outcomes?

EDGING TOWARD
THE CLIFF OF CHANGE

Early in my coaching career, a young client who worked full time and had family responsibilities needed to make some choices about who she was being in order to be considered for advancement in her company. Highly regarded, she was hesitant to speak up when appropriate. Her leaders wanted to see her be more outspoken because they felt she had worthwhile ideas to contribute. I asked her about times in her work life that she had chosen not to speak, even when she had something meaningful to add. We also talked about whether there were other areas outside of work in which she was reluctant to speak. She indicated that her reluctance to speak up was rooted in a broader issue: fear of embarrassment. She worried that her comments might seem out of place or, in more personal situations, that she might in some way cause distress to her children or family. We discussed examples of instances when such fears held her back. She mentioned an activity she wanted to do with her children, but due to her lack of experience with the activity, she feared embarrassing herself in front of her children. This might seem trivial to many people, or even hard to believe, but to her it was important, and it was real. To begin the process of choosing to be more outspoken at work, she decided to take a baby step. The homework she developed for herself was to try the activity without her children a few times to get comfortable with it. She decided to take along a friend who had experience with this activity. One of the things I love about this story is that it reminds us how sometimes baby steps are critical precursors to bigger steps. I was happy when my client reported that she had successfully become comfortable with the activity, and there were some high-fives in our meeting when she told me she had done the activity with her children and that it felt great to have accomplished that goal. This experience was the perfect launchpad for taking a baby step in her work to demonstrate that she had both the desire and the ability to share her opinions and handle more responsibility as a result. She recently embraced just such an opportunity at work that required her to be more confident in expressing her opinions and interacting with others. This client's story reminds me of the old saying about how a journey of a thousand miles begins with the first step. Sometimes jumping off the cliff of change starts by taking small steps toward the edge.

CHAPTER 9

Make a Commitment

It takes a deep commitment to change and an
even deeper commitment to grow.
—RALPH ELLISON

Mike Nelson wrote a book called *Living by Choice: Making the Decisions That Define Your Life.* Originally intended for parents, Mike soon realized the principles he talks about can apply to all adults. He opens the book with this quote from Maurice Switzer's *Letters of a Self-Made Failure:* "You seldom get what you go after unless you know in advance what you want. Indecision has often given advantage to the other fellow because he did his thinking beforehand."

A carefully thought out and intentional choice will sometimes result in temporary failure; however, my experience is that the lack of making intentional choices almost always results in long-term failure and disappointment. Intentional choices do not come with a money-back guarantee, but regrets are almost certain as an outcome of indecision. Borrowing a quote from Babe Ruth, "Every strike brings me closer to the next home run." Great philosophy.

According to Mike Nelson, "Good leaders have an innate *desire* to build something, do something better, and make more out of something. And all of those things apply to an individual's life as well." He talked about three foundational elements in good business decisions/choices.

1. Be honest about the circumstances—don't kid yourself
2. Conduct yourself properly
3. Commit to achieving more

I mentioned earlier that I'd hired Stephen McGhee to be my personal coach. He has helped me in more ways than I could possibly number. Stephen wrote a book entitled *Get Real*, which I think in many ways supports Mike's foundational element of being honest about the circumstances. Sometimes, being honest about the circumstances may be as simple as admitting you must do a lot of ordinary things—every day—to get extraordinary results. For example, one client I worked with periodically found himself unable to find time to think strategically about some important issues. Early on in our work, he discovered if that he would simply book time on his calendar, he would take that time to think about the big picture. For him, if he did the ordinary, basic task of noting it on his calendar, he would always get it done. McGhee says, "I often work with people who want exciting results, but who seek to avoid boring or tedious effort. To these people, I say 'Get real.'"

In my own life, I found this to be true as early as my high school days. If our basketball team lost a game, the next day we would spend most of our practice on some fundamentals of the sport rather than learning new plays. Doing the boring stuff like dribbling down the court or shooting free throws was actually the way to achieve better results.

CONDUCT YOURSELF PROPERLY

A good name is rather to be chosen
than great riches.
—PROVERBS 22:1 (ESV)

If you are a leader, you are watched by everyone around you. The principle in the verse above is largely about choosing between a good name and riches, but has application to all of us regardless of our bank accounts, titles, or ranks. I have seen more promising lives and careers derailed by bad conduct than by lack of skill. You may choose to claw your way to the top or agree to some less than honorable tactics to get you where you want to go, but in the end, such behavior results in failure. Looking at this from a more positive perspective, your impact on others and your business will be magnified by building a reputation for proper conduct in all circumstances.

Often my clients find themselves in situations where they believe they have been wronged or where there is an opportunity to get revenge. There is opportunity for a true leadership moment in every one of these situations, a moment when the best road is the high road. After all, most of us would expect the other person to take the low road. Every time the client has chosen to take the high road (or, exhibit proper conduct), the result of their action left the client feeling really good regardless of the reaction on the other end. Remember, your life is a book. What is the story you want people to read?

COMMIT TO MORE

I want to be sure you give careful thought and reflection about what it really means to commit. I am sure you have heard people explain the difference between involvement and commitment using the story about the chicken and the pig. The story goes something like this: When you have bacon and eggs for breakfast, the chicken is involved but the pig is committed. While I am not suggesting that committing to do more involves dying in a physical sense, it may involve shedding layers of your ego or ceasing to engage in certain behaviors. You may recall that my motivation for writing this book was due, in part, because of the 100 percent success rate I have seen with clients who totally commit to being more of who they are *really* capable of being. Over the length of time I have been working on this book, I have seen even more clients be successful with what they chose to commit to being.

While it's a simple example, I recently worked with an MBA student who was a self-admitted "screen time" junkie. He felt it was adversely affecting his education, and his life in general. He committed to running some experiments to dramatically reduce his screen time. After several weeks, he cut his screen time in half. More importantly, he told me that he learned he could *choose* to be disciplined about a change he wanted to make, and be successful. As Mike Nelson said in our interview, this stuff (committing to do more) works in life as well as business.

Committing to do more opens a world of possibilities that you may never have seen before. "More" has a different meaning for each of us. Examples of commitments to "more" drawn from my clients include:

- Spending time with family
- Taking on less or saying no in order to have time for other priorities
- Bringing your authentic self to the workplace consistently
- Shifting a behavior to become a better leader
- Believing you are capable of being successful at the "next level"
- Stopping behaviors that do not serve you well
- Adopting behaviors that *could* serve you well
- Taking a chance to move toward the next thing, even if the way is not completely clear

As an example of the last bullet point above, sometimes I find that people freeze when trying to decide what should be next or when wondering about the consequences of the next choice. Assuming you have done your homework, the best choice may be to move forward with what you think should be next, while remaining open and observant as you progress. Ask yourself some questions along the way. Do things seem to be falling into place for the direction you want to pursue, or are you encountering obstacle after obstacle? Are there signs that keep pointing you in a different direction and yet you keep ignoring those signs? Pay attention to these things and seek input from others you trust.

When I committed to go to college and then on to graduate school, I had no idea what was even possible for me. All I knew was that I would have a broader array of opportunities available to me if I did go. The list of opportunities that opened to me seems almost endless. I was reminded of these opportunities as I wrote this chapter.

A number of years ago, a business trip took me to Paris for the first time in my life. I asked my wife to go with me so we could stay on after my meetings and be tourists. We certainly got to see many things that we'd thought we would never see, but I remember one particular evening before going out to dinner. While having a cocktail in the lounge at the top of our hotel looking over the city, I turned to my wife and said, "Who would ever have believed that a poor boy from the little town of Hohenwald, Tennessee, would be sitting here at this moment looking at the Eiffel Tower?" Not in a million years would I have thought that would be possible.

What commitments need your attention?

CHAPTER 10

Maintain Balance

I believe that being successful means having a balance of
success stories across the many areas of your life. You can't
truly be considered successful in your business life if your
home life is in shambles.
—ZIG ZIGLAR

I believe that one of the reasons more people don't find
balance in their lives is due to a misunderstanding of what
"balance" really means. My experience is that when you talk
to people about finding balance, they tend to think it means
a fifty-fifty split between work and life. In my own life, and
in what I have observed in others who have what I would call
a balanced life, it is definitely not so evenly divided.

Let me say that I totally understand there will be periods
in your life, or in your work, where the equilibrium must intentionally be out of balance under specific circumstances (a

medical crisis in the family, the birth or adoption of a child, or a temporary upheaval at work, as examples). However, living every day as if there were a crisis is not a sustainable choice. People who seem to live a balanced life have come to understand and commit to being sure that some time is allotted on a regular basis to their faith or whatever feeds them spiritually, family, self-care, and vocation. There is no magic formula for the appropriate amount of time for each, because I believe that is unique to each individual. And the time required for each will likely change during different periods of one's life. But what is critical is a commitment to find the formula that works for you, and to give yourself permission to put some boundaries around each area.

Perhaps you can relate to this: You have been successful at everything you do, so you keep getting asked to do even more. You take that on, and while you try to do everything to the best of your ability, you reach a point of diminishing returns. Or maybe you even experience burnout. Many of us put so much into our work that our health and our personal lives suffer. I can definitely relate. People talk a lot about balance, but I have found that the term really means different things to different people. If you imagine your life to be in balance, what would it look like? I've found that the more specific you can be as you envision such a life, the better the results.

Bob is a great illustration of choosing to be intentional about finding balance. Bob had been a successful salesperson for many years, so, naturally, his employer asked him to lead a team of salespeople. Because he was so successful in that role, he was invited to take on additional leadership responsibilities outside of his local office. Again, he was successful by all of the company's measures. But he found himself working long hours, traveling more, and having limited time for his family. When his company asked him to consider an even bigger role on a national platform, his CEO noticed that Bob was showing signs of significant stress and burnout. He was blessed to have a CEO who was focused on achieving results for the company, but who also cared about each and every one of the individuals under his leadership.

The CEO actually asked me to work with Bob to help him decide who he really wanted to be and how he might develop balance in his life. The initial part of our work together focused on having Bob articulate what he truly enjoyed, what he considered the highest and best use of his time, and what it would take for him to have the time and energy he needed for his family. During this period, Bob and his wife made a commitment to adopt two special needs children. For this to be successful, Bob would need to be more present for the family.

The adoption actually served as a great incentive for Bob to create an infrastructure at work that would allow him to take the time he wanted for his personal life. He achieved this by identifying who could serve at a higher level within his team, being intentional about the delegation of tasks that could be handled by others, and developing trust in his associates' abilities to handle issues in his absence. He also made a commitment to focus on his health. None of this happened overnight, nor was it easy. But Bob was fully committed to making it work.

At the time of this writing, Bob and I have worked together for almost a year. I am happy to report that Bob's team had a record year in terms of sales as well as professional growth of many of the leaders. His traveling commitments have decreased, and he seldom gets home late at night. He and his wife completed the adoption, and he made himself available as needed while his family adjusted to their new members.

As I said earlier, Bob is just one illustration. At its core, the secret to how Bob achieved the balance he identified in advance can be boiled down to his intentionality and commitment. I do not share this illustration to make you think I'm a wonderful coach. I share it because Bob is just one example of how people can achieve something important to them if they are intentional and committed. It is a choice. You can do the same.

I have had clients who have said to me, essentially, "That all sounds very nice, Terry, but there are so many demands on my time there is no way I can get to what you have described as 'balance.'" Like everything else, finding this type of balance starts with a few baby steps, which you could implement even in the next two weeks. Here are examples of the steps some of my clients have utilized to help them in one or more of these areas:

- Putting away the phone at night so it can't be accessed easily, and/or training themselves not to look at their phone until at least half an hour after getting up in the morning
- Changing into exercise clothes right after they get out of bed so they'll feel guilty if they don't exercise
- Adding fifteen to twenty minutes on the calendar for quiet time or meditation first thing in the morning
- Turning off the phone from 5 p.m. until the children go to bed

- Blocking time on the calendar to think longer term
- Scheduling daily time to sit with a spouse, friend, or partner to talk about their respective days
- Stashing their bike gear by the back door so it "stares them in the face" when they walk in from work
- Reviewing emails while waiting for an appointment

As a result of creating even these small steps, clients learned they could indeed find the time to devote to an issue that they previously believed they could not address. I hope you will examine your life, admit there are sectors being neglected, and commit to taking baby steps to giving more attention to those particular interests. Where is your life out of alignment? Sometimes it's necessary to give yourself permission to be out of balance, but don't allow yourself to stay that way.

What is one baby step you could take today to move toward balance in your life?

ENERGY CREATION

What in your life gives you energy? Perhaps it's a hobby, or volunteer work, or a particular aspect of your job. Ask yourself how you might create energy in another area of your life by looking through the lens of what already gives you energy. Let me provide two examples.

I was asked to work with a regional CEO for a large global company because he seemed to have difficulty connecting with a segment of people under his leadership. When we first met, we spent some time talking about his life both at and outside of work. I learned that he coached a baseball team for young children. When I asked him to tell me about this experience, he rose to his feet. His gestures exhibited quite a lot of enthusiasm. He said it was important to understand each child as different, and to work with the individual in order to create a strong team and to help them develop.

When he finished his story, I asked about the difference between how he worked with the young people as a team and how he worked with the people in his office. The lightbulb went off, as it were. He realized right then and there that, other than age, there was no difference between what it takes to build a strong team on the baseball field or in his office. He needed to consider each individual at work, just as he did on the field. He needed to help them develop and to interconnect their skillsets. The key was changing his perspective. He came to understand that he could be energized at work simply by employing the same skills he used with the baseball team.

CHAPTER 11

Face Fear

You gain strength, courage, and confidence by every experience in which you really stop to look fear in the face . . . . You must do the thing you think you cannot do.

—Eleanor Roosevelt

How people behave in groups is an interesting dynamic. Have you observed, in group meetings or discussions, that some people never speak up and others monopolize the conversation? There are probably a few who say little unless they have something timely or thoughtful to share. If one end of the scale is rarely providing input and the other is dominating the meeting, where do you fall?

In my coaching, I have worked with people on the extremes of this continuum. It might surprise you to know that many people in executive positions fear asking questions or giving opinions because they worry about sounding uninformed. On the other extreme, I have coached people who felt they needed to be the smartest person in the room, regardless of the setting. Choosing either extreme does not help the organization or the team dynamics.

Reluctance to Speak Up

Let's first address those of you who may be afraid to speak up in a group for fear of not sounding smart enough. This tendency seems especially prevalent when people are new to a subject or organization, are in a group of intellectual peers, or are not as high on the organizational ladder as others in a meeting.

I have been coaching first-year MBA students for a number of years, and I find this to be a common topic in our early sessions. Despite being admitted to a school with high academic expectations, some students hesitate to speak up in class. At first, I could not comprehend how these smart young people could ever be afraid of saying something unintelligent. But what I did not realize is that often this is the first time in their lives in which everyone around them is on the same intellectual level.

I've also worked with leaders who are comfortable speaking up in any meeting of a peer group, but reluctant to speak when senior management is present. I have even known top-tier salespeople, who are otherwise unafraid to speak to anyone, begin to tremble if asked to speak to a group of other highly successful salespeople.

If you are among those who are reluctant to speak up, what are some strategies to help you get past your reluctance? Like almost every behavioral shift, you need to begin with small steps in order to gain confidence that your input is valuable. Here are a couple of approaches I have seen work with my clients.

Make a commitment to yourself that, for the next three meetings in which you would normally be reluctant to speak up, you will either ask a question or offer a suggestion and observe the reaction of other attendees. Did anyone tell you it was a stupid question or that your comment made absolutely no sense? Did anyone indicate it was a good question or an interesting idea? After the three-meeting experiment, reflect on how you felt after providing input, and think about whether it really was as difficult to speak up as you had imagined.

To raise the experiment to the next level, talk to someone who is likely to be in the same meetings with you. Tell them you are working on speaking up more and ask them if they would be willing to provide honest, direct feedback on your input after the next one or two meetings.

Develop a predetermined set of questions and look for an opportunity to ask one of those questions in the next meeting. To begin developing this list, think about meetings you've been in recently and consider the questions that were asked. Rephrase those questions using your own language and your own voice. Here are a few examples of generic questions that could be applied in almost any industry or meeting:

- I would like to understand more about what you have proposed—can you tell me more about how you arrived at that conclusion?
- What do you think would happen if we tried_____?
- What might be our greatest challenge with implementation?

- We've had some great discussion about this, but what have we overlooked?
- I confess I am relatively new to this topic (or company, group, project), but what if_____?

Capture the list in a notebook, on your phone, or on your tablet and have it available during your next few meetings. Have the list in front of you in an inconspicuous place where you can easily glance at it. Find an opportunity to ask one of your questions and see how it feels.

With some people, I have found that the key to speaking up when they are the most junior person on the organizational ladder requires a shift in their perspective. I had a client who was given a seat in a recurring meeting of primarily operations-oriented executives. She was reluctant to speak due to her lack of operations experience. I asked her how she came to be in the meeting in the first place. Turns out the CEO had invited her. The logical next question was, if the expectation was that she would offer no input, why would she be included in the meeting? Here is where her perspective began to shift, as she realized the CEO must have thought she had ideas or knowledge that might benefit the team. "How might you be cheating your company by not offering your input?" I asked.

She began to see that, even as a novice with regard to operations, her insights might bring a new approach that would add real value. I had spoken with her CEO when our coaching process began, and one of his goals was for her to speak up more in the executive meetings. My client followed the process described above to develop the courage to speak up in meetings. Over the next few months, she found it became easier to offer her input, and she got great feed-back from the CEO and her peers with regard to her fresh perspective. This is just another example of how choosing to look at something from a different angle can make all the difference.

SMARTEST PERSON IN THE ROOM

At the other end of this continuum are those described as "always needing to be the smartest person in the room." I suspect you have worked with people about whom you feel this label is appropriate. I have known a few people who intentionally tried to make others feel stupid or who behaved poorly out of self-interest. I have also worked with people who have earned this moniker but are unaware of their reputation. I have coached a few people of the latter type, and these clients have had amazing problem-solving abilities.

As I've mentioned, I use an assessment tool called the Judgment Index in my coaching practice. Problem-solving is one of the judgment indicators measured by this tool. What I have learned is that people with strong problem-solving skills typically lose patience with those who do not have similar skills. For almost any skill we have that is especially strong, there is a potential blind spot in how we deal with people who do not possess that same level of expertise.

People with strong problem-solving skills tend to have such confidence in their solutions that they find it easier to provide answers themselves than to let others contribute. As a leader, offering all the solutions can derail a career. Subordinates and peers can become frustrated or shut down because they feel the leader has already found a solution and is not open to additional opinions. This is another place where changing the behavior first requires a shift of perspective in a couple of different ways.

One move you need to make is from "I have a good solution" to "Input from others might provide an even better solution." If you are a leader, the other shift may occur when you realize that by having all the answers, you're not allowing others to develop and grow their own gifts and talents.

Two of my former clients come to mind as a way to illustrate this. Though they were completely different in age, role, and industry at the time we worked together, there were many similarities in that the image they projected was off-putting. Both felt that others weren't solving problems quickly enough, and that it was more productive simply to go ahead and solve the problem themselves and then get people working on the solution they'd decided on. Both had aspirations of top leadership roles, but their managers felt their styles were holding them back. Here are the primary actions they took to change.

In one situation, it seemed appropriate for the leader to open up and be a little vulnerable in front of his team. At their next meeting, he announced that he was working with me to become a better leader. He noted that one of his areas of focus was shifting his behavior toward helping them solve their own problems rather than simply providing all the solutions. By saying this out loud, he communicated that he was determined to change. He also gave them permission to call him out when he reverted to his old style of having all the answers. This took a lot of courage, but he was committed.

The other client took a slightly different approach and chose to use me as his accountability partner. The client agreed to conduct an experiment over two weeks. He was to select one of the people with whom he worked on a regular basis, and give that person permission to call him out if he was guilty of automatically solving a problem. During these two weeks, his goal was to make himself pause when his co-worker presented an issue, and to ask for her thoughts on how to deal with it. Because this was a new way of behaving, he knew he might need to help her create her own solutions by giving her more time or by explaining to her how he thought about issues. The two weeks would not be sufficient to totally shift his style, but it gave him the opportunity to watch the positive reactions when he gave others the chance to solve their own problems.

After several months, both clients successfully made the shifts in behavior. Both learned that there are definitely times when they might need to solve a problem for the team in a quick fashion. The majority of situations, however, could be handled appropriately through guiding others to solve their own problems. This, in turn, allowed the leaders to focus their thinking on the bigger picture.

Whether you are on the reluctant or the overbearing end of the continuum, the strategies for changing are similar: be intentional about change; develop some baby steps to move toward the change; find someone to hold you accountable for the change; and notice and celebrate your growth.

Of course, not every choice we make will be easy. Todd Jones told me a story about a difficult choice he had to make when his employer offered him the opportunity to relocate. At the time, he and his family were living near his parents and enjoying the support structure that came along with it. At first, it seemed that there were only two choices: continue living near his family and decline the new assignment presented to him; or make the move and disrupt the support that his family received from his parents. Instead, he and his wife decided that he would commute. Over the years, his career took off, and he had multiple roles that required a long commute. His family has no regrets. Not an easy choice, by any means, but one that was right for them.

When we make choices with the full awareness that sticking with them might be difficult, the odds of being successful are much better.

You may be reading this and saying to yourself, "This guy makes it sound like overcoming bad decisions is not really that hard." But I know it is, in reality. We all have embedded stories we tell ourselves, that only serve to limit us. It can be hard work to create *new* stories, but we must give ourselves permission to do so. Some people are better than others at granting themselves such permission.

Often in my coaching, there will come a moment when I strongly encourage my clients to give themselves permission to do something that is good for them. Todd told me a story of a time when remembering a past mistake had him frozen while trying to make an important decision. Thanks to the good counsel of his wife, who urged him to make his decision based on what he really wanted instead of worrying about what others might want, Todd was able to make up his mind with clarity. The decision came with a potential of significant risk, but with her encouragement, he made the choice that has proven to be one of the best moves of his life. We need permission, courage, and commitment surrounding us when making big choices.

There is so much to be gained by choosing to work on

what may seem difficult, as opposed to what seems easy. Many good lessons will come from the effort, not the least of which is the confidence you will need when having to confront difficult situations in the future. Knowing that we have accomplished difficult things in the past provides courage and confidence in the future.

Where is fear holding you back?

CHAPTER 12

Learn to Listen

*The most important thing in communication
is hearing what isn't said.*
—PETER DRUCKER

One characteristic I have observed about great leaders is that they are great listeners. For much of my career, true listening was an essential skill. Whether I was working with doctors to help hospitals create marketing plans, interviewing clients for a financial services firm, leading large groups of people, or coaching executives, listening skills have been critical.

The International Coaching Federation has a set of eleven core competencies you must demonstrate to be certified as a coach. At least four of the eleven, in part or in whole, relate to listening.

1. Coaching presence: Ability to be fully conscious and

create a spontaneous relationship with the client, employing a style that is open, flexible, and confident

2. Active listening: Ability to focus completely on what the client is saying and is not saying; understand the meaning of what is said in the context of the client's desires; and support the client in self-expression

3. Powerful questioning: Ability to ask questions that review all the information needed for maximum benefit to the coaching relationship and the client

4. Direct communication: Ability to communicate effectively during coaching sessions, and to use language that has the greatest positive impact on the client

If you are not a coach, you may be wondering if this discussion is pertinent to you. I submit that these directives are relevant to all of us, because they speak to characteristics of being a good listener, which all of us need to be regardless of our careers. If I were to put these competencies in everyday language, I would say, "Be fully present in every conversation, pay attention to what is said and not said, and ask clarifying and open-ended questions."

Throughout my career, I've had a number of different roles in which being a good listener was an essential skill. In one of my corporate jobs, I was responsible for getting feedback from clients all over the United States and the United Kingdom. Over the course of about ten years, I conducted face-to-face interviews with more than one thousand clients. The purpose of the interviews was to get a good understanding of what they valued from a financial services firm like ours, and to understand how we were performing. These interviews were appreciated by the clients and highly valued by my company's leadership, resulting in improved business retention. For me, the interviews provided an opportunity to spend time with a variety of interesting people and at the same time learn a lot about effective listening. Drawing on stories from these interviews, my list of effective listening skills includes these eight principles:

1. *Be present in the conversation.* Many times, I conducted up to four client interviews in one day, and typically they were spaced all over the city. So, in addition to the one-hour interviews, I had to build in travel time. Some days were quite rushed, but it was critical that I be fully present in each new conversation and not distracted by thinking about another interview or planning the route I would take to my next appointment in order to avoid traffic. It was vital that I interact fully with each client, and that each client sense my undivided interest and attention.

2. *Signal your engagement with your body language.* Whether you realize it or not, your body language communicates a lot. People can get a sense of your involvement in the conversation by the way you sit or stand, and whether you look at them when they speak. For those interviews, I tried to sit with a relaxed posture, while always looking directly at the client when he or she spoke. If I asked a thought-provoking question, I intentionally looked away for a short period as the interviewee processed a response.

3. *Watch the other person's body language.* Good listeners

understand that people communicate in different ways simultaneously. One of those ways is through their body language. This is one of the primary reasons I insisted on face-to-face interviews if possible. There are hundreds of examples why this was important in the interview. My classic example comes from an interview with a large client. The interview started well, and the client was welcoming and appreciative of the opportunity. But I began to notice that, as he answered my questions, he held some papers in his hand. He pulled on those papers from each side as if trying to release a large amount of pressure from his body. I was concerned that he was stressed while trying to appear cordial in answering my questions. I put down my questionnaire and looked at the client and said, "Is there something going on with you, and if so, could we talk about it?" With that invitation, he spent the next thirty minutes exploding with major frustration about our company and his own workplace. I listened carefully, as he did not seem merely to be bashing other people. I am happy to report that my company immediately took action, made changes, and retained his business. If I had done that interview on the phone, I suspect I would have gotten my questions answered, but I doubt I would have picked up on the hint that we were close to being fired.

4. *Listen actively.* Ask clarifying questions or paraphrase what you have heard, to be sure you have heard correctly. If the other person says that's not what they meant, ask them to restate it in a different way. I

especially found this helpful when listening to people who tended to get off topic easily. If I was interviewing someone who had difficulty staying focused, I would try not to interrupt, but would periodically say something like, "I just want to be sure I am clear about what you were saying. May I tell you what I think I heard?"

5. *Do not interrupt except to clarify.* It may be that you need to let the speaker know you're unclear in what's being said and ask for clarification before proceeding.

6. *Do not give advice or offer solutions if that is not what is being requested.* The few times I ignored this suggestion and instead offered comments about how the company could fix the situation, I discovered my solution was not what they wanted. Instead, they needed me to hear the solution they had come up with on their own.

7. *Do not engage in a conversation with the end already in mind.* We are all guilty of waiting for the moment in a conversation when we can interject our own brilliance. A variation on this happens when we reach conclusions before we have all the facts. People can sense when this is happening, and they may start to clam up in response.

8. *Follow through on any commitments you make.* If you say you will follow up on something, then by all means do it, or explain why you can't. I met with a number of clients who said that their account person from our company did not listen. When I asked for

clarification around why they felt the person was not listening, they all said something along the lines of "because they come and look at us and act like they hear us, but then no action takes place." Lack of follow through after conversations is an especially big pitfall for leaders. People lose trust in leaders who don't do what they say they will do.

I used a number of client interview examples to illustrate the characteristics of effective listening, but the same characteristics apply to conversations in general. Go through each tip listed above and give serious thought to how others might score you if asked to rate your listening skills in a similar manner. Ask a trusted friend or co-worker to give their opinions and see if there are areas that need your attention.

How can you be a better listener?

CRISIS OF CONFIDENCE

People often assume that because someone has a big job with an impressive-sounding title, he or she must be very self-confident. This is not always true. One of my clients is the perfect example. He had risen to an important job in a large company, but for a lot of reasons felt he needed to leave the company and do something different. He was looking for a new kind of challenge. Like many of us, he may have been guilty of running *away* from something rather than toward something. In the end, his new situation was not as expected, and he chose to step out.

When we began to work together, he had moved to another opportunity more aligned with his experience and his interests. His new role allowed him to shine, and he had already proven himself in many different areas. Yet, his personal struggle was to regain his confidence. I refer to this as regaining his "swagger." His memories of what he did not like about the first role he'd left, and his feeling of making a big mistake by going to the next role, weighed heavily on him and caused a crisis of confidence. He knew he didn't want to remain stuck in that place.

Like every other shift or change we need to make, it is important to begin with baby steps. First, I asked him to think back over his career and consider how often his major decisions were wrong. He realized that the vast majority of his decisions had been good, so the probability of making bad decisions was actually pretty low. In this case, we identified a few areas where he could experiment with what happened when he was intentional about speaking with confidence. After a few weeks of "testing," he gained his confidence back regarding his decision-making.

We all have crises of confidence. Accept these as inevitable, but don't let them consume you.

CHAPTER 13

Move from Here and Now to There and Then

Progress is impossible without change, and those who cannot change their minds cannot change anything.
—George Bernard Shaw

When I was attending Coach U to be formally trained as an executive coach, we were taught several different coaching models. The one I liked best was called the "Strategizing for Success" model. I think of it as "here and now" to "there and then." The artist side of my brain was thinking about how I could help myself and my clients visualize how one goes from "here and now" to "there and then."

On the table in our classroom was a stack of multi-colored pipe cleaners. As the instructor talked us through this model, the idea of framing a house (remember, my dad was a carpenter) seemed to resonate as an illustration, so I proceeded to construct a little house frame with the pipe cleaners. To this day, the model hangs in my office as a reminder of the training.

I created this diagram to illustrate a way of moving from where you find yourself today to where you would like to be. Most people understand a simple house diagram. We all know that a house must be built on a solid foundation, have stable walls to create rooms, and be topped off with a strong roof.

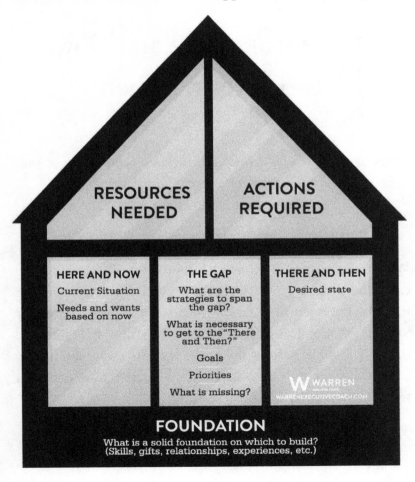

I want you to believe it is possible for you to make changes in your life in order to meet your aspirations and goals. You can choose to move from "here and now" (or, current state) to "there and then" (or, desired state). Ask yourself, "What is possible now?" For some, the choice that needs to be made is a big one. Choosing to shift your thinking from success to significance is large in scope and impact, for example. For others, the needed shift might seem smaller, such as spending less time online. Either way, the changes matter.

Recently, I was on a call with a client who, like so many others, works from home during the COVID-19 outbreak. She was struggling with setting boundaries between her work and her home life because both occurred at the same location, twenty-four hours a day. After a discussion about what it would look like for her to create boundaries and shift her perspective such that she could mentally leave the office and go home, she decided to get in her car and drive to the office, and then come back home to signal the start of the workday. She also created a ritual at the end of the day to symbolize leaving the office and returning home. While we never actually talked about the model or the meaning, through visualizing her desired state, she realized she could do this. She said in hindsight that it was so logical, she wasn't sure why she hadn't thought of it sooner; and she described the decision to set boundaries as life altering.

Remember, there are many types of choices:

- To be confident
- To change who you are being
- To find balance
- To have a different management style

- To be a better person
- To do something you once thought impossible
- To not remain a victim
- To leave a meaningful legacy

When considering what choices you need to make, ask yourself:

- What is really holding you back?
- What would life be like if you were successful with your choices?
- What will life be like if you do not make the choice?
- What needs to change about who you are being?
- How can you change what you are doing, but not change who you are?

As you consider the changes you need to make, remember that knowing yourself is key. You can better understand your personality and your motivations through assessment tools and talking with people who know you well. What energizes you? What compels you to go out into the world? Think about what your life might be like if you make the change you're considering. What would it look like if you stay put? In the end, you must believe you can be successful with your choice.

With any major life change, there's a cost. That cost might be dismantling the belief that if you don't work eighty hours a week you'll never get ahead. The cost might be social. For example, you may have to let go of a relationship in order to reduce negativity in your life. Or the cost may be behavioral, requiring you to resist your natural inclination toward being reserved and instead become more assertive in conversation to make your opinions known. Once you have decided on the change and are at peace with the cost, commit to the choice. Accountability partners can help you with this.

Most importantly, perhaps, think about what it will cost you if you don't make the change. Be willing to let go of the fear. All of us make mistakes, but the most successful of us "fail forward" and learn something along the way. You'll probably experience some discomfort when making a change, but it won't last forever.

Throughout this book I have shared stories that I hope have resonated with you on some level. In these final pages, I offer one more.

In 2019, I was approached about doing a commissioned painting to document a little-known story in our nation's military history. On October 25, 1967, Lieutenant Colonel Gene Smith was flying a mission over Hanoi, Vietnam, when his plane was shot down. He ejected his seat, opened his parachute, threw away his revolver, and smoked a cigarette on his descent. When he hit the ground, he was shot in the leg and captured by the North Vietnamese. After a week of interrogation, he was tossed into a cell, and thus began a five-and-a-half year stay as a prisoner of war in Hoa Lo Prison, which became known as the "Hanoi Hilton." Many pilots and other POWs were in Hanoi Hilton at the same time, including the late Senator John McCain, who was shot down the same month as Lt. Col. Smith. All the POWs endured many years in almost unimaginable circumstances. In order to undermine their will to survive, they were told that America didn't care about them. But the North Vietnamese greatly underestimated the resolve of these heroes.

Then something special happened in May 1972 that provided a bit of hope that these men needed to keep going until their release. It turned out that America had not forgotten them, and other pilots who were aware of the plight of these men were especially attentive. One of those pilots was Lt. Col. John Chancellor.

John told me about that sunny day in May when he and his wingman, flying F-4 Phantom jets, "buzzed" the Hanoi Hilton (flew a few hundred feet above the ground at very high speed) to send a signal to the POWs that their country was with them. With John as lead pilot, flying reconnaissance planes with no serious air-to-ground weapons, they made one pass over the prison and received enemy fire. Then they made a turn and came back for another pass. This time around, John thought it would be "a good idea" for him to do a "roll over" as he made his second pass over the prison. He turned on his afterburners, which catapulted them out of the area at very high speed and also produced sound and reverberation that was unmistakable to the prisoners and felt by everyone.

Gene Smith said to me about that flyover, "This gave us hope to finish out our time as prisoners."

Fast forward to an evening in Mississippi in 1986. Both Gene and John happened to be at the same dinner party. They had never met, and did not know they shared a past: one as a POW at the Hanoi Hilton, and the other as one of the pilots who buzzed the prison. Their time together that night came to a close with gratitude and celebration.

Later, when I had the honor of meeting these men, I asked Gene how he was able to endure five and half years as a POW.

"Trust in God, trust in my country, and trust in my

family," he said. I also asked him to tell me in only a few words what that flyover meant to him. His response was, "It gave us hope."

POW Gene's choice was to stay alive in dire circumstances. He was determined that he would live, despite the conditions. John made a choice that came with great risk. He decided to do something to make the POWs know that their fellow soldiers and their nation cared. He was willing to risk his life to do that.

The choices you need to make may seem like nothing compared to the choices of these brave men, but they are very important to you. For me, making choices and being intentional about seeing them through have an essential ingredient list: faith and trust in God; "cheerleaders" in my network; accountability partners; and belief in myself.

Not everyone will consider what the highest and best use of their time might be when facing a career change. Perhaps for you, the choices have been simple because they sounded like fun or seemed like the right thing to do at the time. If, however, you are someone who relies on deep reflection during those times, then you may want to ask yourself such questions as: "What do I want to leave as a legacy in my work or in my life? Which path will afford me the greatest opportunity to have an impact on the greatest number of people?"

In closing, I invite you to trust your own abilities, all the while having faith in something outside yourself. Have hope! What a powerful word. My hope for you is, after reading this book, you will believe it is possible for you to successfully make the choices you want or need to make. May God bless you and keep you, and give you peace.

FOR FURTHER REFLECTION

When you're contemplating any change, ask yourself:

- What is possible now that was not possible before?
- To make a change/shift, what would I need to stop believing? What would I need to start believing?
- With regard to the stories I tell myself, which of those need to be changed?

When you want to develop your leadership skills, ask yourself:

- What characteristics do I admire most about leaders who inspire me (great speaker, good decision-making, skillful artist)?
- What characteristics do I least admire? What do I want to be sure I don't do?
- What are the primary gaps between my current skills/ behaviors and theirs?
- What do I need to learn or be able to do that I am not doing today?
- Where might I go to develop my skills? Who can help me?

- Who could I speak with that I have observed to always be growing (a relative, friend, leader) and ask how they approached lifelong learning?

When you're thinking long-term or thinking about the future you want, ask yourself:

- What would have to be present for me to have my ideal future state?
- What do I *not* want to be present in my ideal future state?
- How would I describe my ideal future state (salary, place of residence, family life)?
- What needs to fill the gap between my current state and future state?

RECOMMENDED RESOURCES

BOOKS

Bharwaney, Geetu. 2015. *Emotional Resilience.* Harlow, UK: Pearson.

Glaser, Judith. 2016. *Conversational Intelligence: How Great Leaders Build Trust and Get Extraordinary Results.* Philadelphia: Routledge.

Goldsmith, Marshall, and Mark Reiter. 2015. *Triggers.* New York: Hachette.

The Holy Bible, English Standard Version. 2001. Wheaton: Crossway.

Lencioni, Patrick. 2002. *The Five Dysfunctions of a Team.* San Francisco: Jossey-Bass.

Manby, Joel. 2012. *Love Works.* Grand Rapids: Zondervan.

McKeown, Greg. 2014. *Essentialism: The Disciplined Pursuit of Less.* New York: Crown.

Vaden, Rory. 2012. *Take the Stairs: 7 Steps to Achieving True Success.* New York: Penguin.

Wiseman, Liz, and Greg McKeown. 2010. *Multipliers: How the Best Leaders Make Everyone Smarter.* New York: HarperCollins.

ARTICLES AND WEBSITES

Butler, Helen Joy. "Balance Is a Choice, Not a Dirty Word." January 6, 2018. https://balancebydeborahhutton.com. au/balance-choice-not-dirty-word/.

Cazettes, Fanny. "How the Brain Makes Choices." *The Conversation.* December 19, 2018. https:// theconversation.com/how-the-brain-makes-choices- the-sinuous-path-from-decision-to-action-108190.

Chen, Walter. "How to Rewire Your Brain for Positivity and Happiness." *Buffer Blog.* January 31, 2016. https:// buffer.com/resources/how-to-rewire-your-brains-for- positivity-and-happiness/.

The CreatingWe Institute. https://creatingwe.com.

Harrell, Keith. "Why Your Attitude Is Everything." *Success.* September 22, 2016. https://www.success.com/ why-your-attitude-is-everything/.

Holdgraf, Chris. "Decisions in the Brain." *Berkeley Neuroscience News*. June 15, 2015. https://neuroscience. berkeley.edu/decisions-in-the-brain/.

Lee, Daeyeol, PhD, C. Daniel Salzman, MD, PhD, and Xiao-Jing Wang, PhD. "The Neuroscience of Making Decisions." The Kavli Foundation, August 2011. https://www.kavlifoundation.org/science-spotlights/ neuroscience-of-decision-making#.YBxQmi9h3fY.

Conway, Byron. "The 7 Learning Styles: What's Your Learning Style? https://employeeconnect.com/blog/ seven-7-learning-styles/

WORKS CITED

CHAPTER OPENING QUOTES

BrainyQuote. https://www.brainyquote.com.

CHAPTER 1

Buford, Bob. 1997. *Halftime: Changing Your Game Plan from Success to Significance.* Grand Rapids: Zondervan.

"Sully" Sullenberger, Chesley, and Jeffrey Zaslow. 2010. *Highest Duty: My Search for What Really Matters.* New York: William Morrow.

CHAPTER 2

Belmont University. "Belmont at a Glance." https://belmont.edu/.

Daniels, Charlie. 2018. *Let's All Make the Day Count: The Everyday Wisdom of Charlie Daniels.* Nashville: Thomas Nelson, 112.

Goldsmith, Marshall, and Mark Reiter. 2007. *What Got You Here Won't Get You There.* New York: Hachette, 26, 143-46.

The Holy Bible, English Standard Version. 2001. Wheaton: Crossway.

Shakespeare, William. *The Tragedy of Hamlet, Prince of Denmark*. Open Source Shakespeare. https://www. opensourceshakespeare.org/views/plays/play_view. php?WorkID=hamlet&A.

CHAPTER 3

Cooper, Barry. "Beware the God of Open Options." *Christian Living*. TGC, January 28, 2020. https://www. thegospelcoalition.org/article/god-open-options/.

Molloy, John. 1988, *Dress for Success*. New York: Warner.

CHAPTER 5

Patterson, Kerry, Joseph Grenny, Ron McMillan, and Al Switzler. 2012. *Crucial Conversations: Tools for Talking When the Stakes Are High*. New York: McGraw-Hill.

CHAPTER 6

Duhigg, Charles. 2014. *The Power of Habit*. New York: Random House, 32.

CHAPTER 7

Albert, Greg. 2007. *The Simple Secret to a Better Painting: How to Immediately Improve Your Art with This One Rule of Composition*. Cincinnati: North Light Books, 100-01.

CHAPTER 8

Bergland, Christopher. "The Neuroscience of Making a Decision." May 6, 2015. http://www. psychologytoday.com/us/blog/the-athletes-way/201505/ the-neuroscience-making-decision.

Villarica, Hans. https://www.theatlantic.com/health/ archive/2012/04/how-the-power-of-positive-thinking-won-scientific-credibility/256223/

Eurich, Tasha. 2018. *Insight: The Surprising Truth About How Others See Us, How We See Ourselves, and Why the Answers Matter More Than We Think*. New York: Crown, 101, 119.

Fredrickson, Barbara L. "The Broaden–and–Build Theory of Positive Emotions." Philosophical Transactions of the Royal Society of London. Series B: Biological Sciences 359, no. 1449 (September 29, 2004): 1367–77. www.ncbi.nlm.nih.gov/pmc/articles/PMC1693418/ pdf/15347528.pdf

Patoine, Brenda. "The Mindful Brain: Clinical Applications and Mechanistic Clues of Mindfulness Meditation Progress." Dana Foundation, May 30, 2019. https:// www.dana.org/article/the-mindful-brain/.

Peterson, Eugene H. 2005. *The Message*. Colorado Springs: NavPress.

Rudorf, Sarah, and Todd A. Hare. "Interactions between Dorsolateral and Ventromedial Prefrontal Cortex Underlie Context-Dependent Stimulus Valuation in Goal-Directed Choice." Journal of Neuroscience 34, no. 48 (November 26, 2014): 15988–96. https://doi.org/10.1523/jneurosci.3192-14.2014.

Vincent Peale, Norman. 1952. *The Power of Positive Thinking*. New York: Prentice-Hall.

CHAPTER 9

The Holy Bible, English Standard Version. 2001. Wheaton: Crossway.

McGhee, Stephen. 2014. *Get Real: A Vital Breakthrough on Your Life and Leadership*. Denver: Stephen McGhee Leadership. 35.

Nelson, Michael L. 2018. *Living by Choice: Making the Decisions That Define Your Life*. Harrisonburg: Good Choice, 2-3.

CHAPTER 12

International Coaching Federation. https://coachingfederation.org.